马王堆
*Mawangdui*
*Medical*
*Culture*

医学文化
（汉英对照）

(Bilingual Version in Chinese and English)

何清湖——主编

全国百佳图书出版单位
中国中医药出版社
·北京·

**图书在版编目（CIP）数据**

马王堆医学文化：汉英对照 / 何清湖主编.

北京：中国中医药出版社，2024.10

ISBN 978-7-5132-8962-7

Ⅰ. K878.84；R-05

中国国家版本馆CIP数据核字第2024PZ0022号

---

**中国中医药出版社出版**

北京经济技术开发区科创十三街 31 号院二区 8 号楼

邮政编码　100176

传真　010-64405721

北京盛通印刷股份有限公司印刷

各地新华书店经销

开本 787×1092　1/16　印张 10　字数 164 千字

2024 年 10 月第 1 版　2024 年 10 月第 1 次印刷

书号　ISBN 978 - 7 - 5132 - 8962 - 7

定价　100.00 元

网址　www.cptcm.com

服 务 热 线　010-64405510

购 书 热 线　010-89535836

维 权 打 假　010-64405753

微信服务号　zgzyycbs

微商城网址　https://kdt.im/LIdUGr

官 方 微 博　http://e.weibo.com/cptcm

天猫旗舰店网址　https://zgzyycbs.tmall.com

如有印装质量问题请与本社出版部联系（010-64405510）

# 前言

## Preface

在中国考古学界一直流行着这样一个说法，叫作"北有兵马俑，南有马王堆"。1972 年初至 1974 年初，马王堆汉墓出土了 3000 余件文物，惊艳世界，成为闻名中外的历史文化遗产和地标。马王堆汉墓出土文物保存之完好、器物之多样、制作之精致、内涵之丰富前所未有，至今仍是衡量中国汉初社会发展的实物标杆。作为珍贵的历史文化瑰宝，2013 年马王堆汉墓列入第七批全国重点文物保护单位名单，2016 年被评为世界十大古墓稀世珍宝之一，2021 年入选全国"百年百大考古发现"。

马王堆汉墓出土的 15 种古医书及与医学相关的中药、器具等，构成了马王堆医学文化的主要内容。学界考证发现，多部出土医书的成书年代早于《黄帝内经》，是目前保留和重现中国古代早期医学发展水平的最真实、最直接的证据，因而具有重要的文化探源意义和医学传承价值。马王堆医学文化地域特色显著、民生内涵深厚、人文色彩鲜明，蕴含注重生命、注重民生、注重实用、注重生态四大价值取向，表现出"取之于民，用之于民"的独特文化内涵，保持着与时俱进、兼容并蓄的开放品质，是中国地域中医药文化的典型代表和资源宝库。作为湖湘中医药文化的金字招牌，马王堆医学文化具有超越古今、跨越中西的永恒魅力，值得大力传承、弘扬和创新发展。

In the field of Chinese archaeology, there is a popular saying, "In the north lie the Terracotta Warriors, and in the south stands Mawangdui." The Mawangdui Han Dynasty Tombs, which yielded over 3,000 cultural relics between early 1972 and early 1974, have captivated the world and established themselves as a renowned historical and cultural heritage site. These cultural relics are remarkable for their exceptional preservation, wide variety, exquisite craftsmanship, and deep significance. Until now, they are still considered a key benchmark for understanding the social development in China during the Western Han Dynasty ( 202 B.C.—A.D. 8 ). The Mawangdui Han Dynasty Tombs, as a priceless historical treasure, were included in the seventh batch of National Key Cultural Relics Protection Units in 2013, named one of the top 10 rare treasures among ancient tombs worldwide in 2016, and recognized as one of China's "Top 100 Archaeological Discoveries of the Century" in 2021.

The 15 ancient medical books unearthed from the Mawangdui Han Dynasty Tombs, along with the Chinese herbal medicines and medical equipment, form the core of Mawangdui medical heritage. Research has revealed that many of these books predate the *Huangdi's Classic of Medicine*, making them some of the most authentic and direct evidence of early medical practices in China. They hold immense cultural and scholarly value for understanding the development of ancient Chinese medicine (CM). The Mawangdui medical culture carried by these books is characterized by prominent regional features, significant implications for people's well-being, and a rich humanistic dimension. It reflects four major value orientations: a focus on life, people's livelihood, practical usefulness, and ecological balance. The medical culture not only originates from and serves the people, but also embraces an open and evolving spirit, integrating both tradition and innovation. As a shining example of Hunan's traditional Chinese culture, the Mawangdui medical heritage transcends time and cultural boundaries, offering timeless appeal that bridges ancient and modern, Chinese and Western perspectives. It deserves vigorous preservation, promotion, and continued innovation.

中医药作为中华传统文化对外交流互鉴的重要窗口，当前已传播至196个国家和地区，成为中国与世界各国共同增进健康和人类福祉、维护世界和平、构建人类命运共同体的重要载体。为了大力推进中医药融入"一带一路"倡议，需要深入开展中医药"海外传播"行动。马王堆医学文化依托世界知名历史文化遗产马王堆汉墓，具有跨文化传播的影响力。2024年，正值马王堆汉墓发掘50周年，特编写了《马王堆医学文化》这部汉英对照科普图书。本书以精微的语言勾勒出马王堆汉墓的历史人文知识及其丰富的医学文化主体轮廓和特色内容，为国内外中国文化爱好者和中医药爱好者打开一扇走近马王堆医学文化的窗户。同时，期待以"中国文化走出去"为先导，凝聚海内外研究力量推动马王堆医学的研究、交流和转化，以底蕴深厚、源远流长的湖湘中医药文化为人类的健康福祉贡献一份力量。

As a vital bridge for intercultural communication of traditional Chinese culture, CM has now reached 196 countries and regions, emerging as a significant medium for China and the global community to collaboratively advance health, promote well-being, maintain world peace, and build a shared future for humanity. To deeply carry out the intercultural communication of CM and vigorously integrate CM into the Belt and Road Initiative, it is essential to prioritize the international promotion of CM culture.

The Mawangdui Han Dynasty Tombs, with their world-renowned historical and cultural significance, embody the medical culture with considerable cross-cultural influence and recognition. In 2024, marking the 50th anniversary of the discovery of cultural relics from the Mawangdui Han Dynasty Tombs, we have published the bilingual popular science book, the *Mawangdui Medical Culture*, in both Chinese and English. This book provides an accessible yet insightful overview of the historical and cultural context of the Mawangdui Han Dynasty Tombs and explores the main contours and distinctive features of its rich medical heritage. It offers a gateway for enthusiasts of Chinese culture and CM, both domestically and internationally, to delve into the treasures of Mawangdui medical culture.

We hope that by promoting culture internationally, we can attract research collaboration from both domestic and international scholars, fostering further study, exchange, and application of Mawangdui medical culture. By doing these, we aim to contribute to global health and well-being with the profound and enduring medical heritage of Hunan Province.

　　《马王堆医学文化》共十章，图文并茂，通俗易懂，汉英对照是本书的特色。其中，第一章至第三章，通过生动鲜活、引人入胜的历史故事呈现马王堆汉墓的发现和挖掘过程。同时，以马王堆汉墓出土的十五种古医书为主线，将马王堆医学文化的概貌、产生背景、思想特色及核心理念等娓娓道来，帮助读者获得一种整体性和鸟瞰式的认知。第四章至第十章，系统介绍马王堆医学所蕴含的七大具有代表性的医药学理论及其方法、技术、成就，具体包括经络与针砭、导引功法、药物方剂、饮食养生、起居调摄、心理养生和房中养生。上述章节深入浅出地论述了马王堆出土医书及与医学相关的中药、器具等所承载的丰富的知识、理念、方法及其当代价值和启示，构成了全书的主体部分。

　　《马王堆医学文化》由湖湘中医文化研究的首倡者何清湖教授全面指导，陈洪、魏一苇负责编撰和统稿，张冀东、胡以仁、胡宗仁、傅馨莹共同参与中文编写工作。为了便于不同语言背景的读者阅读和理解，本书采用汉英对照的编写方式。由丁颖、杨江担任主译的译者团队为本书的翻译付出了辛勤劳动和不懈努力，在此深表谢意。

The *Mawangdui Medical Culture* comprises 10 chapters, featuring a blend of text and illustrations, easy–to–understand language, and simultaneous Chinese–English comparison.

**Chapters 1 to 3** present the discovery and excavation process of the Mawangdui Han Dynasty Tombs with vivid and captivating historical stories. Additionally, these chapters focus on the 15 ancient medical books unearthed from the Mawangdui Han Dynasty Tombs, providing an overview, background, ideological characteristics, and core concepts of Mawangdui medical culture, helping readers gain a holistic and comprehensive understanding.

**Chapters 4 to 10** systematically introduce seven representative fields of medical theory and their methodological and technological achievements of Mawangdui medical culture. These fields include meridian and colleterals, acupuncture and moxibustion, daoyin exercises, medicinal formulas, dietary regimen, daily life regulation, psychological health preservation, and sexual health preservation. These chapters offer in–depth discussions on the rich knowledge, concepts, methods, as well as contemporary values and insights carried by the medical books unearthed from Mawangdui, along with the related Chinese herbal medicines and equipment, forming the main part of the book.

The *Mawangdui Medical Culture* has been comprehensively guided by Professor He Qinghu, the initiator of Hunan CM culture research, with Chen Hong, Ding Ying and Wei Yiwei responsible for the Chinese writing work. To facilitate reading and understanding by readers from different language backgrounds, we adopt a simultaneous Chinese–English comparison format. The translation team led by Ding Ying, and Yang Jiang has put in diligent work and persistent efforts.

　　《马王堆医学文化》一书向读者展现了大量珍贵的历史图片资料和馆藏文物图片资料，大大提高了图书的知识性、体验性和美观性。在此，特别感谢湖南博物院对本书的图片资料收集给予的大力支持和帮助。为了确保文字资料的准确性，本书在编写过程中广泛阅读了国内有关马王堆汉墓文化研究的权威著作。比如，马王堆汉墓发掘的亲历者，原湖南博物院副馆长傅举有先生所著的《亲历中国考古——马王堆汉墓》，以及马王堆汉墓发掘的亲历者，原湖南省文物考古研究所所长何介钧先生所著的《20世纪中国文物考古发现与研究丛书——马王堆汉墓》，等等。本书在编写过程中参考、吸纳了国内外相关专家学者的研究成果，在此表示衷心的感谢。

　　马王堆医学文化的智慧不仅属于中国，更属于全世界。期待《马王堆医学文化》一书能够架起一座连接东西方医学的桥梁，促进不同文化之间的交流与融合。相信在未来，马王堆医学文化不仅在构建人类命运共同体中发挥桥梁作用，还可以在打造人类卫生健康共同体的道路上越走越远，为全人类的健康卫生事业贡献更多的中国智慧和力量。

何清湖

2024 年 7 月于长沙

The *Mawangdui Medical Culture* presents readers a wealth of precious historical materials and photos of cultural relics from museum collections, significantly enhancing the book's knowledge, experience, and aesthetic appeal. Special thanks are extended to the Hunan Provincial Museum for its strong support and assistance in the collection of image materials for this book.

To ensure the accuracy of the textual information, we have extensively consulted authoritative works on the cultural research of the Mawangdui Han Dynasty Tombs in China during its compilation process. Notable examples include the *Personal Experience of Chinese Archaeology: The Mawangdui Han Dynasty Tombs* by Fu Juyou, a former deputy director of the Hunan Provincial Museum who personally participated in the excavation of the Mawangdui Han Dynasty Tombs, and the *20th Century Cultural Archaeology Discoveries and Research Series: The Mawangdui Han Dynasty Tombs* by He Jiejun, a former director of the Hunan Provincial Institute of Cultural Relics and Archaeology who also participated in the excavation. We also reference and incorporate research findings from relevant experts and scholars both domestically and internationally, and we extend our heartfelt gratitude to them.

The wisdom of Mawangdui medical culture belongs not only to China but to all humanity. It is hoped that the *Mawangdui Medical Culture* will serve as a bridge connecting Eastern and Western medicine, promoting communication and integration between different cultures. In the future, it is believed that Mawangdui medical culture will not only play a bridging role in building a community with a shared future for mankind, but will also make greater strides towards creating a global health community. It will contribute more Chinese wisdom and strength to the health and hygiene endeavors of all humanity.

He Qinghu

July 2024, in Changsha

# 说明 编写

# **Notes on Translation**

在您翻开这本译作之前，我谨代表译者团队，向您致以最诚挚的问候。在此，我想就本次的翻译原则、翻译任务分配、术语翻译原则、翻译目的等，向您做一简要介绍。

在翻译过程中，我们遵循"忠实原作、注重表达"的原则，力求在保持原作文化内涵的同时，使译文更加符合英文表达习惯。我们进行了大量的资料查阅与讨论，在深入研读与理解原作的基础之上，对原作进行了逐句逐段的翻译，力求找到最恰当的英文表达方式。我们尤其注重中医药专业术语的准确性、中国文化的可理解性，充分关注文化差异及其调适问题，力求使译文既准确又流畅。

《马王堆医学文化》（汉英对照）一书的翻译工作由湖湘中医文化研究的首倡者何清湖教授全面指导，丁颖统筹、总校，丁颖、杨江、盛洁、何晓斓、宋梅、胡以仁负责具体的书稿翻译工作。

Before you delve into this translated work, I, on behalf of the translation team, would like to extend our sincerest greetings. Allow me to briefly introduce our translation principles, task allocation, principles for translating terms, and the purpose of the translation work.

We adhere to the principles of "faithfulness to the original text and emphasis on expression", striving to make the translation conform to English expression habits while preserving the cultural connotations of the original work. We conduct extensive research and discussions, translating sentence by sentence and paragraph by paragraph based on a deep understanding of the original text, in an effort to find the most appropriate English expressions. We particularly focus on the accuracy of professional terminology related to Chinese medicine (CM), the comprehensibility of Chinese culture, and adequately address issues of cultural difference adaptation, striving to make the translation both accurate and fluent.

The English manuscript of the *Mawangdui Medical Culture* has been comprehensively guided by Professor He Qinghu, the initiator of Hunan CM culture research, with Ding Ying responsible for overseeing coordination and general proofreading. The translation work has been jointly undertaken by Ding Ying, Yang Jiang, Sheng Jie, He Xiaolan, Song Mei, and Hu Yiren.

## 编写说明 **Notes on Translation**

　　本书中医药专业术语英译一般遵循《世界卫生组织中医术语国际标准（2022 版）》（以下简称《标准》）。对《标准》中存在歧义的某些术语，本书进行了调整。例如，对"标本"一词，本书未采用标准中"tip"和"root"的译法，而是采用"manifestation"和"root cause"，以便英语母语读者更清晰、更直观地理解术语的意义。关于"中医"的翻译，《标准》同时采用"Traditional Chinese Medicine"和"Chinese Medicine"。鉴于中医实践一直随着历史和时代的发展而不断继承、创新和发展，添加"Traditional"一词容易造成误解。因此本书使用"Chinese Medicine"的全称和"CM"的缩写来翻译"中医"。在英文文本中，中药名称以拼音加拉丁语的形式呈现。对一些文化负载词，我们通过正文解释（导引等）和脚注阐述（祝由、信期绣等）相结合的方式，使读者可以更加全面地理解这些文化负载词的含义和背景，从而更深入地领略文本所蕴含的文化内涵。

The English translation of CM terms generally follow the *WHO International Standard Terminologies on Traditional Medicine in the Western Pacific Region: Traditional Chinese Medicine (2022 Edition)*. However, we do diverge occasionally from those terms. For example, as to the term "标本" (manifestation and root cause), instead of using the translations "tip" and "root" provided in the *Standard*, we adopt "manifestation" and "root cause" to enable English native speakers to understand the meaning of the term more clearly and intuitively. Regarding the translation of "中医", both "Traditional Chinese Medicine" and "Chinese Medicine" are used in the *Standard*. Given that the CM practice has been continuously innovated, evolved, and developed throughout history, adding the word "Traditional" can easily lead to misunderstandings. Therefore, the full term "Chinese Medicine" and the abbreviation "CM" are used to translate "中医"in this book. In the English part, the names of Chinese herbs are presented in the form of pinyin plus Latin. For some culturally loaded terms, we adopt a combined approach of inline explanations (such as daoyin) and footnotes (such as Zhuyou, Xinqi embroidery) to enable you to gain a more comprehensive understanding of the meanings and backgrounds of these terms, thereby allowing you to appreciate the cultural connotations embedded in the book to a deeper extent.

目前，影响力最大的马王堆汉墓医书译本由芝加哥大学东亚语言与文明系教授 Donald Harper（夏德安）先生所著。夏德安教授在 1983 年于加州大学伯克利分校获得东方语言学博士学位，其博士论文就是关于马王堆三号墓的医学文献《五十二病方》的研究。后来，在 1998 年，他出版了《早期中国的医学文献：马王堆医学手稿》（*Early Chinese Medical Literature: The Mawangdui Medical Manuscripts*）。这是第一部将马王堆三号墓所有医学文献翻译成西方语言的著作。我们参考了他的较多译法，又对部分表达进行了修改。以马王堆三号墓出土的十五种古医书书名为例，夏德安译本中《脉法》翻译为 *Model of the Vessels*，本书调整为 *Treatment Methods based on Meridians*。前者与脉相关的书名，脉均译为 "vessel"，而本书调整为 "meridian"。《胎产书》被译为 *Book of the Generation of the Fetus*，而我们使用的是 *The Book of Obstetrics*，因为这本书既介绍了胚胎的形成，也介绍了产后保健。

Currently, the most influential translation of the medical books in the Mawangdui Han Dynasty Tombs is authored by Professor Donald Harper, who teaches at the Department of East Asian Languages and Civilizations in the University of Chicago. Professor Harper obtained his doctoral degree in Oriental Linguistics from the University of California, Berkeley in 1983, with his doctoral thesis focusing on the medical book *Formulas for Fifty-two Diseases* in Mawangdui Han Dynasty Tomb 3. Later, in 1998, he published the *Early Chinese Medical Literature: The Mawangdui Medical Manuscripts*, which was the first work to translate all the medical books from Mawangdui Han Dynasty Tomb 3 into a Western language. We have referenced many of his translations but have also made modifications to some. Taking the names of the 15 ancient medical books excavated from Tomb 3 as an example, in Harper's book,《脉法》is translated as *Model of the Vessels*, while we have adjusted it to *Treatment Methods based on Meridians*. As to the book titles related to "脉" in Harper's translation, "脉" is translated as "vessel", while in this book, it has been adjusted to "meridian".《胎产书》is translated as *the Book of the Generation of the Fetus*, while we use the *Book of Obstetrics,* since the book introduces both the formation of embryos and postpartum health care.

最后，我们希望读者在阅读这部书的译作时，能够体会到马王堆医书对世界的意义在于其历史文化价值、学术研究价值、临床实践价值、文化传承价值、教育普及价值等多个方面。这些价值的实现将有助于推动医学理论的发展和创新，丰富医学史的研究资料，弘扬中医文化并促进文化交流与合作。同时，也希望读者能够对我们的翻译工作提出宝贵的意见与建议，以便我们在今后的翻译工作中不断改进与提高。

同时，我们也得到了中文作者、相关专家和编辑的宝贵建议与帮助，在此向他们表示衷心的感谢。

愿这部书的译作能够为您带来思考与启示。

丁颖

2024 年 8 月于长沙

Lastly, we hope that readers will appreciate the significance of the medical books in the Mawangdui Han Dynasty Tombs to the world in terms of their historical and cultural value, academic research value, clinical practice value, cultural heritage value, and educational and popularization value. The realization of these values will contribute to advancing the development and innovation of medical theories, enriching research materials in the history of medicine, promoting CM culture, and fostering cultural exchange and cooperation. We also hope that you will provide valuable feedback and suggestions on our translation work, so that we can continuously improve and enhance our translation efforts in the future.

We have also received valuable advice and assistance from the Chinese authors, relevant experts, and editors, and we express our heartfelt gratitude to them.

May this translation bring you inspiration.

Ding Ying

August 2024, in Changsha

# 目录

## List of Contents

马王堆医学文化的智慧不仅属于中国，
更属于全世界。

在中国这个古老而又现代的东方大国，有一个令人神往的地方，那就是马王堆汉墓。这座充满神秘色彩的西汉墓葬，隐藏着一个数千年的医学文化宝库，等待着被发掘和探索。让我们一起掀开历史的面纱，与这个"世界级的考古奇迹"来一场跨越时空的相遇。

In China, this ancient yet modern oriental country, there is a fascinating place named Mawangdui.The mysterious Western Han Dynasty tombs here conceal a treasure trove of medical culture spanning thousands of years, awaiting being excavated and explored. Now, let's lift the veil of history and have a cross time encounter with the "world-class archaeological miracle".

千年不朽的
东方睡美人

The Millennia Immortal Sleeping
Beauty of the Orient

# 长沙城

　　"天上一颗星，地上长沙城。"作为湖南省省会、特大城市的长沙，位于湖南省东部偏北，坐落在湘江北去与浏阳河的交汇处，因城市对应天上轸宿旁的长沙星而得名。在距今15万～20万年的旧石器时代，长沙地区就有原始人类活动。2500余年城址如一、城名相续的长沙，北接洞庭湖，西屏岳麓山，有江水穿城而过，更有橘子洲浮碧江心。承续源远流长的湖湘文脉，坐拥灿若星河的楚汉古迹。长沙因其深厚的文化底蕴和优美的山水风光，自古便享有"楚汉名城"的美誉。

"The Changsha Star is in the sky, the Changsha City is on the earth." As the capital and mega city, Changsha is situated in the northeast of Hunan Province, where the Xiang River and the Liuyang River intersect. It is named after its correspondence with the Changsha Star next to the Zhen constellation (one of the 28 constellations in ancient Chinese astronomy and mythology). About 150,000—200,000 years ago, humans began to reproduce and thrive here. Changsha has maintained the same city site and continued its name for more than 2,500 years. It is bordered to the north by Dongting Lake and to the west by Yuelu Mountain. The Xiangjiang River runs through the city, with the Orange Island "floating" like an emerald at the heart of the river. Changsha has inherited the long histories of Hunan culture and surrounded by numerous Chu-Han historical relics. Owing to its profound cultural heritage and beautiful scenery, Changsha has enjoyed the reputation of "Renowned City of Chu-Han" since ancient times.

# 马王堆

在长沙市东郊五里牌外，有一座方圆半里的小山。山上有两座高十八九米的大土堆，因为外形很像马的鞍具，当地人称它为"马鞍堆"，后来被讹传为"马王堆"。长期以来，人们认为此处是五代十国时期楚王马殷的家族墓地。据清光绪十四年（1888年）编撰的《湖南全省掌故备考》记载："五代楚王马殷疑冢在省城东北。"也有人提出，马王堆里葬的是西汉汉景帝的妃子唐姬和程姬。比如，明清以来湖南的一些地方志如《湖南通志》等就沿用了这种说法，故又称其为"二姬墓"。那么，历史的真相到底是什么呢？虽然有了史书、方志的记载，但由于没有进行过实地发掘，仍然无法得到确切的结论，马王堆墓主人的这个谜便一直延续了下去。

马王堆汉墓外景
Scene of the Han Tombs at Mawangdui
一、二号墓封土堆东西相联，形似马鞍，故又名"马鞍堆"。
The two mounds of Tombs No.1 and No.2 are linked from east to west in the shape of a saddle, thus Mawangdui has also been called "ma an dui" (saddle mound).

20世纪50年代马王堆外景
Scenery of Mawangdui in the 1950s

Outside Wuli Pai, the eastern suburb of the Changsha City, there is a hill with a radius of 250 meters. On the hill there are two large mounds with a height of 18—19 meters. Due to their resemblance to horse saddles, locals originally called them "Ma'andui" (saddle mounds). For a long time, people believed that this was the family cemetery of Ma Yin, King of the Chu State in the period of the Five Dynasties and Ten Kingdoms (907—979), thereafter it was misrepresented to be "Mawangdui" (mounds of the King Surnamed Ma). According to the *Hunan Province Chronicles Preparation* compiled in 1888, the 14th year of the Guangxu reign of the Qing Dynasty, "the tomb of Ma Yin, King of the Chu State, was suspected to locate in the northeast of Hunan Province." It was suggested as well that Tang Ji and Cheng Ji, two concubines of Emperor Jing of the Western Han Dynasty (202 B.C.—A.D. 8), were buried here. Some local chronicles of Hunan since the Ming and Qing dynasties (1368—1912), such as the *Hunan General Annals*, followed it to call Mawangdui as the "Two Concubines Tomb". Such being the case, what was the truth of history? Although there had been records in historical books and local chronicles, due to the lack of on-site excavation, it was still impossible to draw a definite conclusion. The mystery of the owner of the tombs remained unsolved.

1951 年，中国科学院考古研究所组织了一个长沙考古队，通过对马王堆进行实地勘察和钻探，初步断定这是一处汉代墓葬群，时间要比五代十国的"马殷墓"早一千多年，由此揭开了马王堆不姓"马"的历史面纱。但是，由于受到保护手段和保护技术方面的局限，当时并没有进行发掘。直到 1970 年，当地某部队医院看中了马王堆这处地方，要在这里兴建地下病房和手术室，但在施工过程中，总是遇到奇怪的塌方，并且发现了软质的白膏泥。工人们用钢钎去探查，忽然从钻孔里冒出了呛人的气体，好奇的人用火去点，竟然燃起了蓝色的火苗。这令人惊慌不解的消息，经过三天的辗转，终于幸运地转达到了湖南博物院。根据考古的经验，这种俗称"火洞子"的古墓往往因为保存了大量的沼气，所以封闭十分严实，里边的文物可能保存得比较完好。由于马王堆已经遭到破坏，必须马上进行保护性的科学发掘，经过国务院批准，发掘工作由湖南博物院承担，并于 1972 年 1 月 16 日正式开始启动。

马王堆一号墓挖掘现场
Excavation Site of Mawangdui Han Dynasty Tomb 1

In 1951, a Changsha archaeological team, organized by the Institute of Archaeology of the Chinese Academy of Sciences, conducted a field survey and on-site drilling in Mawangdui. The team preliminarily concluded that it was a Han Dynasty tombs group, dating back more than 1,000 years earlier than the Tomb of Ma Yin in the period of the Five Dynasties and Ten Kingdoms (907—979). This uncovered that the owner of Mawangdui was not surnamed "Ma". However, due to the limitations of protection and techniques, excavation was not implemented until 1970. That year, Mawangdui was spotted by a local military hospital intending to build underground wards and operating rooms there. Unexpectedly, during the construction process, unusual landslides were frequently encountered and soft white plasters were found. As the workers used steel drills to explore, a choking gas suddenly emitted from the drilling hole. Curious workers used fire to light it. To their surprise, it ignited a blue flame. Fortunately, the alarming and confusing news, after three days of twists and turns, finally came to the officials of Hunan Provincial Museum. Archaeological experiences indicated that such tombs, commonly known as "fire holes", often contained a large amount of methane due to tight seal, and the artifacts inside might be relatively well preserved. Due to the former destruction of tombs, protective scientific excavation should be carried out immediately. With the approval of the State Council, excavation work was undertaken by Hunan Provincial Museum and officially commenced on January 16, 1972.

考古工作人员把东边的墓编为一号墓，西边的墓编为二号墓，发掘先从已经遭到破坏的一号墓开始。

由于封土堆体积庞大，墓口规模宏大（墓口长19.5米，宽17.8米），尽管动用了推土机、吊车等先进机械工具，仍是历时近4个月，马王堆一号墓墓主的棺椁才出现在人们面前。这是一个方形的墓，从墓口到墓底深达16米，从上到下像漏斗似的逐渐缩小。清理完墓坑里30多层紧密的五花夯土、厚达1.3米的白膏泥及重达5吨的木炭后，里边露出了26张平铺成4排的嫩黄色竹席。考古人员小心翼翼地掀开这些崭新的竹席，墓坑底部长6.72米、宽4.88米、高2.8米的纯木质结构的椁室出现了，震撼着大家的视野，一号墓的墓主即将浮出水面。考古专家用钢棍撬开第一层盖板和边框后，发现下面还有两层，直至掀开第三层椁盖才真正窥见这座沉睡于地下两千多年的神秘殿堂。"当东方现出朝霞，太阳冉冉升起时，我们打开了北边箱，箱内放着密密麻麻、上下重叠、古里古怪、色彩艳丽的各种随葬器物，一下驱散了考古挖掘人员几天来的困倦与劳累……"这是1972年主持马王堆汉墓发掘工作的熊传薪回忆的当时的场景。

马王堆一号墓挖掘现场
Excavation Site of Mawangdui
Han Dynasty Tomb 1

Archaeological workers labeled the eastern tomb as Tomb 1 and the western one as Tomb 2. The excavation started from Tomb 1, which had already been damaged. Due to the massive grave mound and the grand tomb entrance measuring 19.5 meters in length and 17.8 meters in width, despite the use of advanced mechanical tools such as bulldozers and cranes, it took nearly four months of efforts for the coffin in Tomb 1 to finally appear in front of the world. It was a square tomb, with a depth of 16 meters, gradually shrinking from the top to the bottom like a funnel. After clearing over 30 layers of rammed earth in the grave, along with 1.3-meter-thick mud paste and more than 5,000 kilograms of charcoal, 26 bright yellow bamboo mats were exposed, spreading out in four rows. Archaeologists carefully lifted these brand new bamboo mats. The pure wooden structure of the outer coffin at the bottom of the tomb, measuring 6.72 meters in length, 4.88 meters in width, and 2.8 meters in height, amazed everyone. The owner of Tomb 1 was about to surface. Archaeologists used steel bars to pry open the first layer of covers and frames, only to find that there were two more layers below. It was not until the third layer cover was lifted that the mysterious palace, which had been dormant underground for over 2,000 years, was truly revealed."When the morning glow appeared in the east and the sun slowly rose, we opened the box in the north.It was filled with various funerary objects that were densely packed, overlapping up and down, peculiar and brightly colored. The fatigue and exhaustion of the archaeologists for several days was dispelled at the moment …" This was the scene recalled by Xiong Chuanxin, who presided over the excavation of the Mawangdui Han Dynasty Tombs in 1972.

椁室呈"井"字形结构，古代叫作"井椁"，中间的棺室用以放置层层相套的棺材，四个巨大的边箱则用来放置随葬器物。椁室边箱的布局在一定意义上再现了贵族的宅第，反映了墓主人所处时代"事死如事生"的理念。四个边箱中，北边箱（也就是头箱）最大，这里象征着古人生前居住和活动的场所。四个边箱里层层叠叠堆满了随葬的器物。云纹漆鼎里盛放着千年不朽的藕片，陶罐里装的紫红色杨梅还带着青色果柄，那些光亮如新的漆器、华丽轻柔的丝绸等随葬物品，历经 2000 年的尘封依旧艳丽如新。一桩桩惊喜拨动着考古人员的心弦，那么开棺的那一刻，人们将会见到怎样惊异的景象呢？

The outer coffin had a Chinese character "井 (well)" structure, which was called "well coffin" in ancient times. The middle chamber was used to place layers of nested coffins, and the four huge side-chambers were used to place funerary objects. The layout of the side-chambers in the outer coffin was, in a certain sense, a reproduction of the aristocratic mansion, reflecting the concept of "treating death as life" in the era of the tomb owner. The northern-side-chamber, also known as the head box, the largest of the four, resembled the place where the tomb owner lived during her lifetime. The four side-chambers were stacked layer by layer with funerary objects. The cloud-patterned lacquer tripod held millenium immortal lotus root slices, and the pottery jar contained purple red bayberries with green fruit stalks. The shiny lacquerware, gorgeous and soft silk, and other funerary objects endured 2,000 years of dust but remained as beautiful as new. Surprises stirred the hearts of archaeologists one after another, then what kind of amazing scene would people see when opening the coffin?

马王堆一号墓椁室结构及随葬物展示
Display of the Outer Coffin and Funeral Objects in Tomb 1

13

庞大的棺材打开，外层是庄重的黑漆素棺，没有任何装饰。第二层是黑地彩绘漆棺，黑漆为地，在黑漆地上用金黄色绘出漫卷多变的云气纹，纹路中穿插着一百一十一个神怪、仙人和禽兽，洋溢着浓厚的浪漫主义色彩。第三层是朱地彩绘漆棺，这种被《汉书》记载为通体"内外洞朱"的彩绘漆棺，只有身份很高的贵族才能使用，再次暗示着墓主人的不凡身世。在鲜艳的朱漆地上，用青绿、粉褐、藕褐、赤褐、焕白等颜色彩绘出龙、虎、雀、鹿、仙人、仙山等寓意祥瑞的图案，展现了一派富丽堂皇的气象。第四层是最牵动人心的内棺，棺身涂满黑漆，上面覆盖着长达两米的T形帛画，更令人称奇的是，内棺的四壁板和盖板都以铺绒绣镶边，以羽毛贴花绢为中心装饰。这是考古队首次发现羽衣棺，给内棺穿上羽衣，寄寓着墓主人"羽化而登仙"的美好愿望。而T形帛画在墓中的随葬品清单上被称为"非衣"（因其外形"似衣而非衣"得名），整幅帛画用极富想象力的浪漫手法表达了古人对天国的向往和对永生的追求，寓意墓主人的灵魂将依靠这件"非衣"飞升天国。

马王堆一号墓黑地彩绘漆棺
Coffin with Painted Designs on Black Lacquer Coating in Tomb 1

马王堆一号墓朱地彩绘漆棺
Coffin with Painted Designs on Vermilion Lacquer Coating in Tomb 1

The huge coffin was opened. Its outer layer was a solemn black lacquer coffin without any decoration. Its second layer was a painted coffin, with golden patterns depicting the ever-changing clouds on black lacquer coating. The patterns were interspersed with 111 gods, monsters, immortals, and animals, exuding a strong sense of romanticism. The third layer was the coffin with painted designs on vermilion lacquer coating. On the bright coating, auspicious patterns such as dragons, tigers, sparrows, deer, immortals, and immortal mountains were painted in green, pink brown, purplish gray, reddish brown, and radiant white, showing a magnificent atmosphere and implying the extraordinary status of the tomb owner as well. Such type of coffin, recorded in the *Book of Han* as having a vermilion whole body in the inner and outer, can only be used for high-ranking nobles. The fourth layer was the most exciting inner coffin, with its body painted in black and covered with a 2-meter-long T-shaped painting on silk. Even more remarkable was that the four wall panels and cover plates of the inner coffin were embroidered with velvet edges, decorated with feathered silk in the center. This was the first time an archaeological team had discovered a feathered coffin. An inner coffin adorned with a feathered coat symbolized the beautiful wish of the tomb owner to transmigrate to an immortal through metamorphosis. The T-shaped painting on silk, on the list of funerary objects in the tomb, beared the name "clothes beyond", which was coined due to its appearance resembling clothes but distinct from ordinary clothing. Imaginative and romantic techniques were utilized to express the ancient people's longing for heaven and their pursuit of eternal life, symbolizing that the soul of the tomb owner would soar to heaven with the "clothes beyond".

马王堆一号墓T形帛画
T-shaped Painting on Silk in Tomb 1

要想见到墓主人的真容，还得打开羽衣内棺。1972 年 4 月 28 日，考古专家花了一整天的时间才把密封得非常严实的棺盖揭开，只见墓主人身上包裹着层层严实的丝织品，浸泡在无色透明的棺液之中（出土不久变成棕黄色）。绢绮罗纱锦，春夏秋冬装，剥开这多达二十层的包裹物又耗费了整整一周的时间。揭衣过程中强烈的酸臭味刺激着人们的鼻息，却深深兴奋着考古专家的神经，难道真的有奇迹出现？事实果真惊艳了人们的眼睛——这具身高 1.54 米、体重 60 千克的女尸像是被时光遗忘的睡美人。她的外形完整，肤色淡黄，面色鲜活，发色如真，甚至眼睫毛都清晰可见，几乎与刚刚谢世相差无几。她的多处皮肤软组织柔软而富有弹性，内脏器官完整无损，血管结构清楚，骨质组织完好，部分关节还能够活动，甚至腹内仍存留一些食物。医学检查发现，这位墓室女主人患有多发性胆结石和严重的冠心病，结合其胃肠中残留的一百三十八粒半还未消化的甜瓜瓜子，可以合理推断，她死于胆绞痛诱发的冠心病。这是世界上已发现的保存时间最长的一具湿尸，能如此清晰地了解 2200 年前人类的死因，这在考古史上也是绝无仅有的事情，堪称世界考古史上的奇迹。

马王堆一号墓出土女尸
Female Corpse in Tomb 1

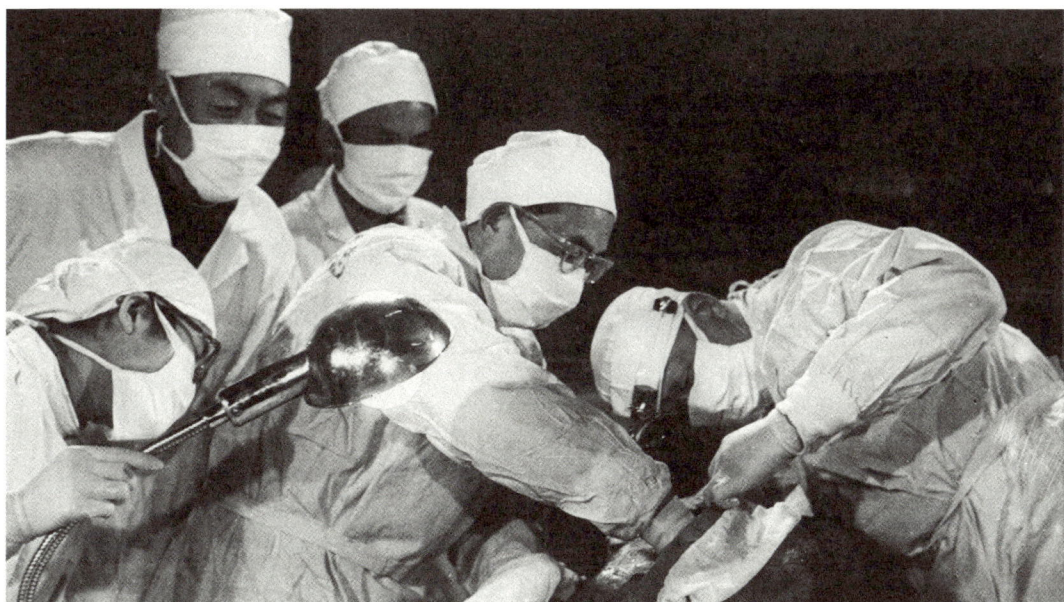

马王堆一号墓出土女尸解剖工作现场
Autopsy Site of the Female Corpse in  Tomb 1

To see the true face of the tomb owner, the feathered inner coffin had to be opened. On April 28, 1972, archaeologists spent a whole day uncovering the tightly sealed lid of the coffin. The tomb owner was wrapped in layers of tightly woven silk and soaked in colorless transparent coffin liquid, which turned tan soon when unearthed. It took another whole week to unwrap the up to 20 layers of the spring, summer, autumn, and winter clothing made of silk, brocade, chiffon, or damask.The strong sour smell during the process of uncovering clothes stimulated breathing, but excited the nerves of archaeologists. Was there really a miracle to happen? The fact did amaze peoples' eyes—the female corpse, standing 1.54 meters tall and weighing 34.5 kilograms, like a sleeping beauty forgotten by time. Her body was intact in appearance, with a light yellow skin tone and a lively complexion. Her hair color was as real as ever, and even her eyelashes were clearly visible, almost indistinguishable from her recent passing. Many parts of the skin were soft and elastic, the internal organs were intact, the blood vessel structure was clear, the bone tissue was intact with some joints still able to move, and even some food was left in the stomach. Medical examination revealed that the female owner of the tomb suffered from multiple gallstones and severe coronary heart disease. Based on the remaining 138 and a half undigested sweet melon seeds in her gastrointestinal tract, it could be reasonably inferred that she died from coronary heart disease induced by biliary colic. This has been the longest preserved wet corpse discovered in the world, and it has been unprecedented in archaeological history to have such a clear understanding of the cause of a human death 2,200 years ago, making it a miracle in the history of world archaeology.

　　一号墓的发掘工作至此基本结束，但是墓室女主人的身份依然是一个谜团。随着文物清理过程中一枚刻着"妾辛追"的印章的发现，东方睡美人的真实身份浮出水面，辛追夫人的名字传遍大江南北，惊艳世界各地。另外，在一些随葬器物上，比如一号墓出土的大量漆器上有朱书"轪侯家"的铭文，缄封着"轪侯家丞"封泥，根据这些实物并结合文献记载推断，此处所葬为某一代轪侯的妻子，由此基本确定墓葬的年代属于西汉初期。而在一号墓的挖掘过程中，意外地发现它的南边还有一个大型汉墓，因此被命名为三号墓。为了进一步弄清真相，1973 年 11 月开启了对马王堆二号墓、三号墓的发掘。遗憾的是，由于三号墓封闭不严、严重渗水，墓主人的尸体及覆盖的衣物只存朽迹，并没有找到关于墓主人身份的明确信息。揭秘的最后希望寄托在二号墓上，由于墓室被毁坏，考古人员不得不在泥水中摸索。忽然有人从淤泥中拣出了两颗印章，分别是刻有阴文篆体"轪侯之印"的龟钮鎏金铜印和刻有阴文篆体"利苍"的私人玉印。根据史书记载，轪侯利苍曾在西汉初年担任长沙国丞相。随着一方刻有阴文篆体"长沙丞相"的龟钮鎏金铜印从椁底板下的淤泥中清洗出来，三个墓葬主人的身份终于有了确切的答案。最早修造的二号墓主人是第一代轪侯利苍，而最晚修造的一号墓则是利苍的妻子辛追。三号墓的主人根据医学测定，是一位三十岁左右的年轻男子，初步推断是利苍和辛追的儿子，但其具体身份仍存在争议。

马王堆一号墓出土的"妾辛追"泥质印章（私章）
Mud Seal Inscribed with "妾辛追 (Concubine Xin Zhui)" in Tomb 1 (Personal Seal)

马王堆二号墓出土的「利苍」玉印（私印）
Jade Seal Inscribed with「利苍(Li Cang)」in Tomb 2 (Personal Seal)

马王堆二号墓出土的「长沙丞相」龟钮鎏金铜印（官印）
Gilded Turtle-Shaped Copper Seal Inscribed with「长沙丞相 (The Prime Minister of Changsha)」in Tomb 2 (Offical Seal)

The excavation work of Tomb 1 had basically came to an end, but the identity of the female owner of the tomb remained a mystery. With the discovery of a seal inscribed with the characters "妾辛追"(Concubine Xin Zhui) in the process of cultural relics sorting, the true identity of the sleeping beauty of the Orient surfaced.And thereafter the name of Xin Zhui spread across China and amazed the world. Besides, on some funerary objects, such as a large number of lacquerware unearthed from Tomb 1, there were the inscriptions of "轪侯家" (Marquis of Dai Family) in vermilion, which were sealed with "轪侯家丞"(Chancellor of the Marquis of Dai Family) seal mud. Based on these funerary objects and combined with literature records, it could be inferred that the wife of a Marquis of Dai was buried here, which basically determined that the burial age belonged to the early Western Han Dynasty. During the excavation of Tomb 1, it was unexpectedly discovered that there was another large Han tomb to the south, thus named Tomb 3. In order to further clarify the facts, the excavation work of Tomb 2 and Tomb 3 began in November 1973. Unfortunately, due to the lax sealing and severe water seepage of Tomb 3, only traces of decay of the corpse and covering clothing of the tomb owner were found, while the identity of the tomb owner remained unknown. The final hope for the revelation lay in Tomb 2.As the tomb chamber was destroyed and archaeologists had to explore in the mud and water. Suddenly, two seals were picked out from the mud, namely the gilded turtle-shaped copper seal engraving seal characters of "轪侯之印"(The Seal of Marquis of Dai) and the private jade seal engraving seal characters of "利苍" (Li Cang), all characters cut in intaglio. According to historical records, Li Cang, the Marquis of Dai, served as the Prime Minister in the Kingdom of Changsha in the early Western Han Dynasty. As another gilded turtle-shaped copper seal inscribed with"长沙丞相" (The Prime Minister of Changsha) was washed out of the mud under the bottom of the outer coffin, the identities of the three tomb owners were finally determined. The owner of Tomb 2 (first built), was Li Cang,the Marquis of Dai, while the owner of Tomb 1 (built the latest), was Xin Zhui, Li Cang's wife. According to medical measurements, the owner of Tomb 3 was a young man around 30 years old. He might be the son of Li Cang and Xin Zhui according to the preliminary inference, but his exact identity remains controversial.

　　这位沉睡了 2200 余年的东方睡美人的身份虽然已经揭晓，但是关于千年不朽的谜团仍在历史迷宫的长廊里流连。直到今天，人们仍在坚持不懈地探寻着辛追夫人的不朽之谜。

The identity of the sleeping beauty of the Orient, who has been sleeping for over 2,200 years, has been revealed, but the mystery of millennia immortality will linger in the long corridor of the historical maze. Until now, people are still persistently exploring the immortal mystery of Xin Zhui, the Lady of Dai.

跨越时空的

# 医学瑰宝

**The Medical Treasure Transcending Time and Space**

　　三号墓的发掘工作伴随着各种转机，让考古人员的心情跌宕起伏。从青灰色白膏泥中挖出的绿叶，宛如刚从树上采摘下来一般鲜嫩，裹入泥中的竹枝青翠欲滴，椁室上面露出的竹席亦泛着嫩黄的新色，这似乎都在传递着振奋人心的消息。最初揭开椁板时，人们发出欢呼，因为发现椁室边箱中盛满了各类保存完好、五光十色的随葬品，墓主人的棺木也十分完整。然而，接下来的发掘却让考古人员担忧不已，墓主人的尸体已腐朽成为骨架。

　　正如中国古代典籍《老子》（又名《道德经》）所言："祸兮福所倚，福兮祸所伏。"失望中往往潜藏着转机和幸运。这位博学多才的年轻墓主虽然没能创造千年不朽的奇迹，但他为后世留下了另一笔珍贵的财富——大量的帛书和医简。这些出土帛书和医书竹、木简存放于三号墓东边箱北端的长方形大漆书奁里。帛书大部分写在宽 48 厘米的整幅帛上，折叠成长方形，放在奁盒下层的一个格子里；小部分则书写在宽 24 厘米的半幅帛上，用木条将其卷起，压在两卷竹简的下面，放在奁盒的长条格里。

马王堆三号墓挖掘现场
Excavation Site of Mawangdui
Han Dynasty Tomb 3

马王堆三号墓出土的漆书奁
Lacquer Book Box in Tomb 3

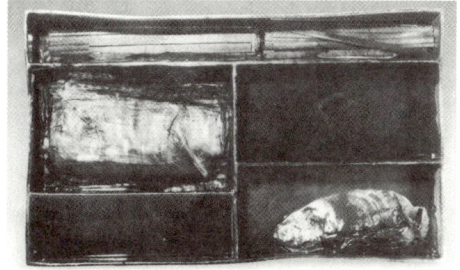

漆书奁存放的医简和帛书
Medical Books on Silk, Bamboo, or Wooden Slips
Kept in Lacquer Book Box

The excavation of Tomb 3 was fraught with twists and turns, and the archaeologists experienced ups and downs.The green leaves dug out from the greenish gray mud paste were as fresh and tender as if they had just been picked from the tree, the bamboo branches wrapped in the mud were lush and dripping and the bamboo mats exposed above the outer coffin were also tinged with a tender yellow new color, all of which seemed to be conveying uplifting news. Thus when the outer coffin was first opened, people cheered, finding that its side-chambers were filled with various well preserved and colorful funerary objects and the tomb owner's coffin was still intact. However, the subsequent excavation gave cause for concern among the archaeologists due to the fact that the tomb owner's body had long decayed into a skeleton.

As stated in the ancient Chinese classic *Tao Te Ching*, "Fortune and misfortune come in turn." Despite being unable to create a millennia-spanning immortal legacy, the knowledgeable and skilled young tomb owner had bestowed upon future generations a profound wealth: an extensive collection of books on silk, bamboo or wooden slips. These unearthed books were stored in a rectangular lacquer box at the northern end of the eastern side-chamber in Tomb 3. Among the books on silk, the majority were written on an entire 48-centimeter-wide piece of silk, which were then folded into a rectangular shape and neatly arranged in a grid at the base of the dressing case; the minority, however, were on a half-sized piece of silk measuring 24 centimeters wide, rolled up with wooden strips, compressed beneath two rolls of bamboo slips, and then placed within the elongated grid of the dressing box.

出土帛书被专家团队整理为 47 种，共计 12 万余字，这是继汉代发现孔府壁中书、晋代发现汲冢竹书及清代发现敦煌经卷之后的又一次重大古代典籍发现。帛书内容以中国古代哲学、历史等社会科学为主，也有相当一部分是自然科学方面的著作，还有多种图籍和杂书，充分反映了中国自战国至西汉初期古代先贤的杰出智慧及深厚的科学人文素养。帛书具体涉及的领域包括哲学、历史、文学、军事、宗教、绘画等，也兼及天文、地理、医学、历法、气象、建筑、畜牧等。大部分帛书内容是已经失传了一两千年的佚本，其中不乏对中国古代著名典籍《周易》《老子》等的抄录，出土帛书《周易》更被认为是现存最早的《周易》抄本之一。这些都表明马王堆汉墓出土帛书对中国古文献学和中国学术史的研究具有极其重要的价值。马王堆一号墓和三号墓还出土了帛画 11 幅、遣策（用于记录随葬物品的清单）722 支、医简 200 支，这批简帛为研究中国古代的科学、文化、医药和绘画艺术各方面提供了十分珍贵的实物资料。

马王堆三号墓出土帛书《老子》抄本（局部图）
Manuscript Copy of the *Tao Te Ching* on Silk in Tomb 3 (Partial Picture)

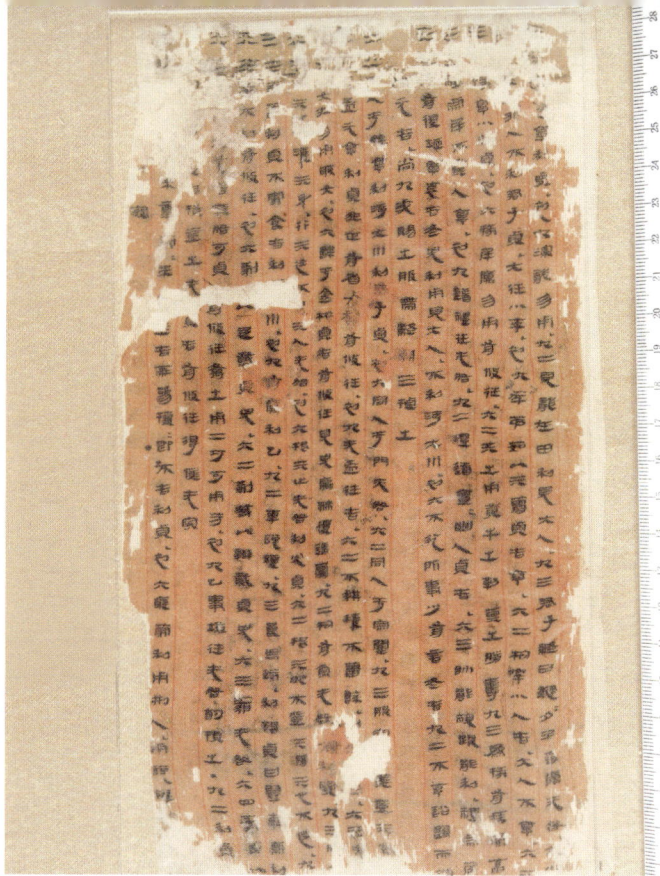

马王堆三号墓出土帛书《周易》抄本（局部图）
Manuscript Copy of the *Book of Changes* on Silk in Tomb 3 (Partial Picture)

The excavated books on silk have been categorized by a team of experts into 47 distinct types, comprising a total of approximately 120,000 characters. This marks the fourth significant discovery of ancient books, following the revelation of the books concealed within the walls of the Confucius Mansion in the Han Dynasty (206 B.C.— A.D. 220), Jizhong Bamboo Books in the Jin Dynasty (266—420), and the Dunhuang Scriptures in the Qing Dynasty (1644—1912). The contents of the books on silk predominantly include ancient Chinese philosophy, history, and various other social sciences, alongside a substantial portion dedicated to works pertaining to natural sciences. There are also various illustrations and miscellaneous books on silk. These books fully reflect the outstanding wisdom and profound scientific and humanistic literacy of ancient Chinese sages from the Warring States period (475—221 B.C.) to the early Western Han Dynasty. The books on silk specifically cover the fields of philosophy, history, literature, military, religion, painting, as well as astronomy, geography, medicine, calendar, meteorology, architecture, and animal husbandry. Most of them contain manuscripts of texts that have been lost for one or two thousand years, including those of famous ancient Chinese classics such as the *Book of Changes* and the *Tao Te Ching*. The unearthed silk manuscript of the *Book of Changes* is regarded as one of the earliest manuscripts of the book extant. This is to indicate, in terms of ancient Chinese literature and academic history, the profound significance of the books on silk discovered in Mawangdui. Besides, 11 paintings on silk, 722 lists of the funerary objects, and 200 bamboo or wooden slips relating to medical contents were unearthed from Tomb 1 and Tomb 3 in Mawangdui. These silks and slips offer invaluable physical materials for delving into the ancient Chinese science, culture, medicine, and the painting art.

此后，对马王堆出土帛书和医简的研究逐渐形成一门独立的学科——马王堆学。而福泽后世的马王堆医学正是通过对这些历久弥新的古籍的传承、创新和发展，展现出跨越时空、超越国界的魅力。经过整理发现，出土帛书、帛画中有医学典籍10种，包括《足臂十一脉灸经》《阴阳十一脉灸经》（因不同抄录版本，分甲乙本），以及《五十二病方》《养生方》《杂疗方》《脉法》《阴阳脉死候》《却谷食气》《胎产书》，还有一幅独特的出土帛画《导引图》。此外，三号墓还出土了两卷简书，包含200支医书竹简和木简。其中，一卷内容与《黄帝内经》相似，讲的是养生之道；另一卷则为房中术。按照医简的内容，经整理分别定名为《天下至道谈》《十问》《合阴阳》和《杂禁方》。除《杂禁方》为11支木简外，其余均为竹简。马王堆三号汉墓出土古医书（简称"马王堆医书"）共计14种。后由湖南博物院、复旦大学出土文献与古文字研究中心编纂的《长沙马王堆汉墓简帛集成》，将《杂疗方》细分成《房内记》和《疗射工毒方》，马王堆医书种类变成15种。据考证，大部分医书的抄录年代是战国末期至西汉文帝十二年（公元前168年）之间，而其著作的年代则更早。因此，马王堆医书的出土刷新了多个中医药学发展史上之"最早"，将中医学理论、方法的发源追溯到先秦时期。

Since then, the research into the excavated books on silk, bamboo, and wooden slips from Mawangdui has gradually evolved into an independent discipline known as Mawangdui Studies. Meanwhile, Mawangdui medicine, a blessing for future generations, shows its timeless and transnational allure through the inheritance, innovation, and further development of these enduring ancient medical books. After careful sorting, 10 medical classics have been discovered, including medical books on silk such as the *Moxibustion Classic of the Eleven Meridians of the Foot and Forearm*, the *Moxibustion Classic of the Eleven Yin-Yang Meridians* (including versions A and B due to different transcription versions), the *Formulas for Fifty-two Diseases*, the *Formulas for Health Preservation*, the *Formulas for Various Cures*, the *Treatment Methods based on Meridians*, the *Death Signs of Yin-Yang Meridians*, the *Avoiding Food Intake and Practising Breathing to Cultivate Qi*, and the *Book of Obstetrics*, as well as a unique painting on silk, the *Drawings of Guiding and Stretching*. In addition, two volumes of medical slips,consisting of 200 bamboo or wooden slips, were unearthed from Tomb 3.Among them, one volume is analogous to the *Huangdi's Classic of Medicine* in terms of contents, primarily focusing on methods of health preservation, while the other volume delves into sexual techniques. According to the contents, the medical slips have been sorted and named as the *Discussion on the Supreme Dao of the World*, the *Ten Questions*, the *Conjoining Yin and Yang*, and the *Formulas for Various Charms* respectively. Except for the 11 wooden slips of the *Formulas for Various Charms*, the medical slips are bamboo slips. A total of 14 ancient medical texts, shortly known as "Mawangdui Medical Books", were found in Tomb 3. The *Collection of Bamboo and Wooden Slips and Silk from the Mawangdui Han Dynasty Tombs in Changsha*, Compiled by members from Hunan Provincial Museum and Fudan University Center for Excavated Documents and Ancient Scripts Research, have subdivided the text titled the *Formulas for Various Cures* into two distinct parts: the *Formulas for Sexual Life* and the *Formulas for Caterpillar Sting Poison*. This subdivision has yielded a total of 15 medical books. According to textual research, the majority of medical books were transcribed between the late Warring States period (476—221 B.C.) and the twelfth year of Emperor Wen of the Western Han Dynasty (168 B.C.), with the original works dating back even earlier. As a consequence, the excavation of Mawangdui medical books has rewritten the "earliest" chapter in the developmental history of Chinese medicine (CM) in China, tracing the origins of Chinese medical theory and practices back to the pre-Qin period (from remote antiquity to 221 B.C.).

帛书抄录的《五十二病方》是一种久已亡佚的医学专著，共一万余字，因卷前目录列有五十二种疾病的标题而得名，现存医方总数为 283 个，用药达 247 种之多，是迄今为止发现的最早的医方书。《五十二病方》卷前还抄录了关于古代医学理论的四种佚书，与之合抄为一卷。其中，《足臂十一脉灸经》是迄今为止最古老的一部经脉学著作，简要论述了人体 11 条经脉的循行部位和涉及的病候，以及以灸法为主的治疗方式，现存文字大部分完整。《阴阳十一脉灸经》甲本抄录在《足臂十一脉灸经》之后，由于与抄录在《导引图》之前的乙本可相互弥补而基本保存完整，其论述的内容也较《足臂十一脉灸经》有了较大的进步和丰富，被视为中国最早的灸疗学著作。《脉法》和《阴阳脉死候》抄录在《阴阳十一脉灸经》甲本的尾部，最早提出了关于人体气与脉的关系及三阴脉、三阳脉疾病死亡征候的相关理论。帛书《养生方》是一部以养生为主的方书，共 32 篇，其中现存可辨识的医方为 88 个，主要用于滋补强壮、增强体力，是中国最早的养生学文献。帛图《导引图》彩绘有 44 个不同运动姿势的人像，展现了古老的导引术的术式并载有相应的名称，是中国迄今发现的最早的健身图谱和气功养生文献。《却谷食气》是抄录于《导引图》之前的佚书，原文无标题，是一部道家思想影响下利用呼吸运动进行个人保健的书籍，亦被视为最早的气功文献材料之一。房中养生学（相当于现代性医学的范畴）是马王堆医书的一个重要组成部分，竹简《十问》《合阴阳》《天下至道谈》及帛书《房内记》都是迄今最早的性医学专著。这些房中养生学著作主要介绍了性生理和性心理，以及关于性机能疾病的防治，在世界性医学方面做出了开拓性贡献。帛书《胎产书》是关于妇女胎产的方技书，通过图文结合的方式介绍了胚胎形成过程、产妇调摄及 20 余个医方，是迄今最早的妇产科学文献。木简《杂禁方》共11 支，每简 13 ～ 14 字，主要讨论怎样运用符咒等法来治疗夫妻不和、妇姑相斗、婴儿啼哭及多噩梦之类的问题，与其他出土医书中的祝由方一起反映了当时祝由疗法的应用疾病、医疗方式及特色。

The book titled the *Formulas for Fifty-two Diseases* is a long-lost medical monograph that comprises over 10,000 characters, documenting valuable insights into ancient medicinal practices. It is aptly named after the 52 diseases enumerated in the comprehensive table of contents featured at the fore of the tome. Being the earliest discovered medical formula book so far, it records a total of 283 existing medical formulas and 247 different medicines. Four lost books on ancient medical theories are also transcribed at the location prior to the *Formulas for Fifty-two Diseases,* with the five being transcribed together into one volume.Among them, the *Moxibustion Classic of the Eleven Meridians of the Foot and Forearm* has been the earliest work so far to study meridians, briefly discussing the circulating regions of 11 meridians in the human body and the related diseases, as well as the treatment methods mainly based on moxibustion. Most of the existing texts in it are complete. The version A of the *Moxibustion Classic of the Eleven Yin-Yang Meridians* is transcribed following the *Moxibustion Classic of the Eleven Meridians of the Foot and Forearm,* and it is basically intact because the version B of it transcribed in front of the *Drawings of Guiding and Stretching* can complement it.Being regarded as the earliest work on moxibustion in China, its contents are more sufficient and plentiful compared to those of the *Moxibustion Classic of the Eleven Meridians of the Foot and Forearm.* The *Treatment Methods based on Meridians* and the *Death Signs of Yin-Yang Meridians* are transcribed after the version A of the *Moxibustion Classic of the Eleven Yin-Yang Meridians,* proposing the earliest theories in China on the relationship between qi and meridians in the body, as well as the death signs of diseases related to the three yin and three yang meridians. The *Formulas for Health Preservation,* transcribed on silk, is a formula book mainly concerning health preservation. Among its 32 chapters, there are 88 identifiable medical formulas extant, mainly used for tonifying and fortifying, and boosting vitality. It is the earliest literature on health preservation in China. The *Drawings of Guiding and Stretching* on silk depicts 44 figures in different postures, demonstrating the ancient techniques of daoyin (guiding and stretching exercises) bearing corresponding names. It is a fitness illustration and literature of qigong health preservation discovered in China to date. The *Avoiding Food Intake and Practising Breathing to Cultivate Qi* is a lost book located in front of the *Drawings of Guiding and Stretching.* The original text, untitled, is a book dedicated to breathing exercises aiming at personal health care, deeply influenced by Taoist philosophy. It is also regarded as one of the earliest qigong literature materials. The preservation of health in the bedroom, which aligns with the domain of modern sexual medicine, constitutes a significant aspect of Mawangdui medical books. The *Ten Questions,*the *Conjoining Yin and Yang,* and the *Discussion on the Supreme Dao of the World,* inscribed on bamboo strips, and the *Formulas for Sexual Life* inscribed on silk, are all among the earliest known specialized works on sexual medicine. These works primarily focus on introducing sexual physiology and psychology, along with the prevention and treatment of sexual dysfunction diseases, thereby making groundbreaking contributions to the sexual medicine worldwide. The *Book of Obstetrics,* transcribed on silk, introduces the formation of embryos, postpartum health care, and over 20 medical formulas through a combination of illustrations and text. It is the earliest scientific literature on obstetrics and gynecology to date. There are additionally 11 wooden slips constituting the *Formulas for Various Charms,* with each slip bearing 13—14 characters. These slips primarily explore techniques for utilizing talismans and charms to address problems such as marital discord, strife between mothers-in-law and daughters-in-law, incessantly crying infants, and frequent nightmares. Together with other excavated medical texts featuring formulas of Zhuyou therapy[1], these slips illustrate the diverse illnesses cured by Zhuyou, the popular practices and distinctive traits of Zhuyou during that era.

---

[1] Zhuyou therapy is the traditional Chinese psychotherapy that emphasizes the use of suggestion and persuasion to treat illnesses.

20 世纪 70 年代以来，随着国内外学界对马王堆汉墓出土的帛书和医简的研究不断深化，经过半个世纪的挖掘、整理、提高和转化，马王堆医学文化已成为中国地域中医药文化的重要组成部分和典型代表。马王堆医学文化对中国传统医学的贡献，不仅局限于养生保健领域，还广泛涵盖养生学、药物学、方剂学、经络针灸学，以及骨伤科、男科、胎产生殖理论、祝由疗法等中医临床各科诊疗知识，为中医经络学、脉学、方药学、保健学及性医学的溯源提供了更为久远的可考文献资料。根据当前学界达成的共识，一般把马王堆医学文化视为中医理论体系化过程中早期成果的总结，尤其对秦汉时期中医理论的发展具有承上启下的作用，被称为后世中医基础理论（尤其是养生学思想）的源头活水。这些经过时光打磨的医学瑰宝透露出历久弥新的内在，它们化作湖湘中医发展源流中的洪流，在历史长河里奔流不息。

Since the 1970s, academic circles at home and abroad have been continuously deepening their research on the books on silk and medical books on bamboo or wooden slips excavated from the Mawangdui Han Dynasty Tombs. With the efforts of excavation, sorting, enhancement, and transformation over the past 50 years, Mawangdui medical culture has emerged as a significant element and exemplary representation of regional CM culture. Transcending the realm of health preservation and healthcare, the contributions of Mawangdui medical culture to CM encompass a wide range of clinical knowledge in CM, such as health preservation, medicines and formulas, meridians, acupuncture and moxibustion, orthopedics and traumatology, andrology, obstetrics and gynecology, Zhuyou therapy, and beyond. Mawangdui medical culture offers ancient and dependable documentary materials vital for tracing the origins of CM theory, pulse diagnosis, pharmacology, healthcare, and sexual medicine. Based on the consensus reached within the academic community, Mawangdui medical culture is widely acknowledged as a compilation of early accomplishments in the systematization of CM theory. It serves as a bridge in the development of CM theory between the Qin and Han dynasties (221 B.C.—A.D. 220), and is recognized as the source of subsequent basic theories in CM, particularly the ideas of health preservation. These medical treasures, polished by time, unveil an everlasting spirit that has evolved into expansive ripples in the development of CM in Hunan, persisting indefinitely in the vast expanse of history.

福泽后世的
# 健康智慧

# The Health Wisdom Benefiting
# Later Generations

湘江

打开历史的封藏，抖落时光的尘埃，以马王堆汉墓出土医书为核心的马王堆医学文化，是湖湘大地的一颗璀璨明珠。独特的自然地理环境，休养生息的民本政治，以及"贵生""尊生"的社会思潮，共同孕育了地域特色显著、民生内涵深厚、人文色彩鲜明的马王堆医学文化。该文化是中华大地地域中医药文化的典范。

As the seal of history is unveiled and the dust of time is shaken off, the Mawangdui medical culture, centered on the unearthed medical books from the Mawangdui Han Dynasty Tombs, emerges as a brilliant pearl on the land of Hunan. The unique natural geographical environment, the people-oriented politics focusing on recuperation, and the social trend of "valuing and respecting life" have jointly nurtured the Mawangdui medical culture with significant regional characteristics, profound connotations of people's well-being, and distinctive humanistic colors, making it a model of regional CM culture across China.

湖南北临洞庭湖，有湘、资、沅、澧四水归汇，自古就有"鱼米之乡"的美誉。同时，湖南属于亚热带季风气候，日照充足，雨量丰富，土地肥沃，四季分明，为动植物提供了良好的生存环境。发达的农耕文明和丰富的物产资源，为人们追求健康生活方式奠定了良好的物质基础。这种自然环境亦宜于中药材的生长、种植和栽培，如湖南涟源龙山自古就有"天下药山""植物王国"的美称。纵观马王堆出土医书，关乎养生的内容几乎占据半数，所用俗文、俗药、俗法皆体现出为民所用的显著特点。马王堆医学文化凸显出深厚的民生内涵，这与西汉初期的民本政治环境密不可分。当时国家实行休养生息和轻徭薄赋的政策，推行"无为而治，从民之欲"的黄老政治，为老百姓创造了宽松、自由、安定的社会环境。这就有助于人们在生活实践中不断积累、总结有利于民力恢复、身体健康、人口繁衍的经验和方法。与此同时，先秦时期诸子百家学术争鸣，养生学说也尤为丰富多彩。其中，黄老学说不仅作用于政治民生领域，也深刻影响着当时的生命和健康观念。道家提倡"贵生""尊生"（即珍惜、尊重生命），确立"返朴归真""虚静无为"的养生理论，主张顺其自然、恬淡虚无、知足常乐的生活态度。而形成于春秋战国时期的阴阳学说，则为马王堆医学文化中房中养生学的理论框架和方法体系奠定了思想基础。概而言之，这些中国古代哲学的思想理念历经养生学家和普通百姓的再创造、再丰富，实现了从哲学观到养生观再到方法论的转化，形成了一系列行之有效的养生方法和技巧，从而构建起马王堆医学文化独特的知识和方法体系。

Hunan has Dongting Lake in the north, where the four rivers—Xiang, Zi, Yuan and Li converge. It has been known as the "land of fish and rice" since ancient times. Furthermore, Hunan enjoys a subtropical monsoonal climate with abundant sunshine, plentiful rainfall, fertile soil, and four distinct seasons, thereby offering an ideal habitat for flora and fauna. The highly developed farming civilization and rich natural resources have laid a solid material foundation for the pursuit of healthy lifestyle. This natural environment is also suitable for the growth, planting, and cultivation of Chinese herbs. For example, Longshan Mountain in Lianyuan City has been regarded as the "Mountain of Medicines" and the "Kingdom of Plants" since ancient times. From a bird's eye view, the contents related to health preservation take up almost half of the medical books unearthed from the Mawangdui Han Dynasty Tombs, and the folk texts, folk medicines, and folk methods employed therein all reflect notable characteristics of being used widespreadly by the people. The Mawangdui medical culture highlights a profound connotation of people's well-being, which is closely related to the people-oriented political environment in the early Western Han Dynasty (202 B.C.—A.D. 8). At that time, the government implemented policies of recuperation and low taxation, and pursued the Huangdi-Laozi politics[2] of "governing by doing nothing that goes against nature and following the desires of the people", creating a relaxed, free, and stable social environment for the people. This helped the people to continuously accumulate and summarize experiences and methods beneficial for the productivity restoration, physical health-maintenance, and population growth in their daily lives. At the same time, the contention of various schools of thought occurred during the pre-Qin period, contributing to the richness of health preservation theories. Among those schools, the dissemination of the combined doctrine of Huangdi and-Laozi not only substantially applied to the fields of politics and people's livelihood, but also profoundly shaped the concepts of life and health at that time. For example, advocating the view of "valuing and respecting life", Taoists developed a health-preserving theory of "returning to original purity and simplicity", "quietism and nothingness", and "letting things take their own course", in favor of the life attitude such as letting it be, being peaceful and indifferent to fame or gain, as well as being contented. Besides, the yin-yang theory, which was formulated during the periods of Spring and Autumn and Warring States (770—221 B.C.), laid the ideological foundation for the establishment of the theoretical framework and methodological system of health preservation on sexual medicine in the Mawangdui medical culture. In summary, these ancient Chinese philosophical ideas have undergone the recreation and reenrichment by health preservation scholars and ordinary people, and have been transformed from philosophical views into health preservation views and then into the methodologies, forming a series of effective health preservation methods and techniques, thus constructing a unique knowledge and method system of Mawangdui medical culture.

---

[2] Huangdi-Laozi politics refer to the political views from the combined doctrine of Huangdi and Laozi. The combined doctrine of Huangdi and Laozi originated from the Warring States Period (476—221 B.C.), and flourished in the Western Han Dynasty (202 B.C.—A.D. 8). In the names of Huangdi and Laozi, this doctrine combines the theory of Taoist School and Legalism, and also includes the yin-yang theory, Confucianism, Mohism, etc. It carries forward the thought of Tao, holding that "Tao" is the ultimate noumenon and objective principle in nature that man should follow. It emphasizes on "governing by doing nothing that goes against nature".

　　"精、气、神"被称为天、地、人三才之道中的"人身之三要"，一直被中国古人誉为"人身三宝"。三者相互联系，精充可以化气，气盛可以全神，神全则阴阳平衡、脏腑协调、气血畅达。因此，"聚精、养气、存神"是健康长寿、防病治病的根本。马王堆医书对我国先秦到西汉时期的养生保健理论和防病治病方法，进行了最早的、较全面的记载和论述，各篇都涉及了"精""气""神"这些字眼。其中，以《十问》对三者的论述最为体系化，其次是《养生方》《却谷食气》《阴阳脉死候》等篇目。这三个字也经常组合为"神气""精气""精神"等。"聚精"方面，马王堆医学主张"食养生精"和"房中守精"，即通过饮食调摄和节欲守精来达到保养阴精的目的。"养气"方面，马王堆医书《脉法》首次提出了"寒头煖（暖）足"的养生原则，主张通过遵循人体阴经、阳经的循行规律来培养科学的起居习惯。导引亦是加强人体气血功能活动的重要保健方法。"存神"思想散见于马王堆古医书之中，如《十问》主张要神和内得、精神和谐，这样才能精力充沛、五脏固健、容颜焕发，从而达到强身、健体、长寿的目的。概而言之，马王堆医学虽然尚未形成完整的精、气、神系统性理论思想，但其中所蕴含的古老医学智慧无不体现出对人身精、气、神的重视，为后世精、气、神医学思想的发展奠定了坚实的基础。

马王堆三号墓出土医简
《十问》（局部图）
The *Ten Questions* on
Bamboo Strips in Tomb 3
(Partial Picture)

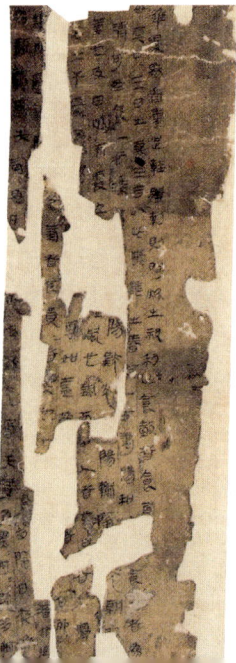

马王堆三号墓出土帛书
《却谷食气》（局部图）
Silk Manuscript of the
*Avoiding Food Intake and
Practising Breathing to
Cultivate Qi* in Tomb 3
(Partial Picture)

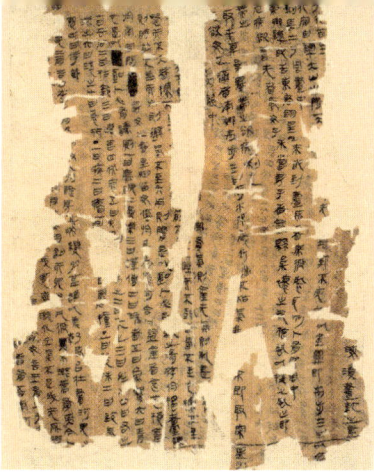

马王堆三号墓出土帛书《养生方》（局部图）
Silk Manuscript of the *Formulas for Health Preservation* in Tomb 3
(Partial Picture)

"Essence, qi, and spirit" are known as the "three essentials of a man" in the three elements of heaven, earth, and human beings, and have always been praised as the "three treasures of life" by ancient Chinese people. The three are interrelated. Sufficient essence can transform into qi; abundant qi ensures normal function of the spirit, which in turn balances yin and yang, coordinates zang-fu organs, and facilitates the smooth flow of qi and blood. Therefore, "preserving essence", "cultivating qi", and "harmonizing spirit"are fundamental to health and longevity, as well as disease prevention and treatment. The Mawangdui medical books provide the earliest and most comprehensive records and discussions on health preservation theories and disease prevention and treatment methods from the pre-Qin period to the Western Han Dynasty (202 B.C.—8 A.D.) in China. Each article involves the characters "气(qi)", "精(essence)", and "神(spirit)". However,the discussions on these three characters in the *Ten Questions* are the most systematic, followed by the *Formulas for Health Preservation*, the *Avoiding Food Intake and Practising Breathing to Cultivate Qi*, and the *Death Signs of Yin-Yang Meridians*. Moreover, they are often combined as "神气(shen qi)" "精气(jing qi)" and "精神(jing shen)"[3], etc. In terms of "preserving essence", Mawangdui medicine advocates"generating essence by food"and "preserving essence through controlled sexual intercourse", i.e. one should preserve yin-essence by dietary regulation and continence. In terms of "cultivating qi", the medical book *Treatment Methods based on Meridians* for the first time has proposed the health preservation principle of "keeping the head cold and the feet warm", holding that the circulating laws of the yin and yang meridians of the human body should be followed to cultivate scientific living habits. Additionally, daoyin is an important health preservation method for enhancing the functional activities of the body's qi and blood. And the idea of "harmonizing spirit" can also be found in the Mawangdui medical books. For example, the *Ten Questions* advocates that the harmony of the spirit ensures the full energy, the consolidated and healthy five zang organs, and a radiant complexion, so as to achieve the goals of strengthening the body, improving health, and prolonging life. In summary, although Mawangdui medicine has not yet formed a complete theoretical framework of essence, qi, and spirit, its ancient medical insights reflect the emphasis on them, which thereby has paved a strong groundwork for the development of medical thoughts on essence, qi, and spirit in later generations.

---

[3] "神气(shen qi)" "精气(jing qi)" and "精神(jing shen)" are not translated into English here, because the meanings of the three words differ in specific contexts.

除养生学思想以外，药物学、方剂学成就也是马王堆医学文化留给后世的宝贵医学遗产。有研究发现，马王堆医书共记载矿物药 31 种、植物药 169 种、谷类药 18 种、菜类药 10 种，同时还包括用药的时间与禁忌等相关知识，突出反映了春秋战国时期中国药物学的发展。《五十二病方》《养生方》《杂禁方》《疗射工毒方》记载了较为丰富的方剂学内容。尤其是《五十二病方》，存医方 283 首，用药 247 种，所用剂型达十数种；使用病名约 103 个，涉及内、外、妇产、小儿、五官科等方面。该书涉及疾病分类、方剂组成、制剂、煎服法、用法、禁忌、治法治则、复方配伍、辨证论治等内容，"理、法、方、药"主轴线已初具雏形。其方剂组成以一二味药物为多，从所载内容中可知，此期已是方剂学的萌芽时期，反映了该领域由零散记载向系统化、专门化整理过渡的真实情况。

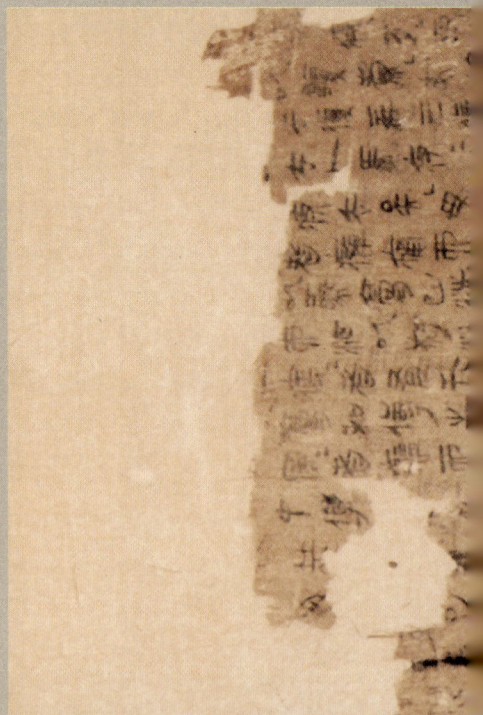

马王堆三号墓出土帛书《五十二病方》（局部图）
Silk Manuscript of the *Formulas for Fifty-two Diseases* in Tomb 3 (Partial Picture)

In addition to the philosophy of health preservation, the achievements in Chinese medicines and formulas are also valuable medical legacies left by the Mawangdui medical culture to future generations. Research has found that the Mawangdui medical books records a total of 31 mineral medicines, 169 herbal medicines, 18 cereal medicines, and 10 types of vegetable medicines, as well as related knowledge about the timing and contraindications of medication, which represents the development of Chinese pharmacology during the periods of Spring and Autumn and Warring States (770—221 B.C.). The *Formulas for Fifty-two Diseases*, the *Formulas for Health Preservation*, the *Formulas for Various Charms*, and the *Formulas for Caterpillar Sting Poison* record a wealth of Chinese medicinal formulas. Particularly in the *Formulas for Fifty-two Diseases*, there are 283 existing formulas, involving 247 Chinese medicines and more than 10 dosage forms; about 103 disease names are used, involving the diseases of internal medicine, external medicine, obstetrics and gynecology, pediatrics, ophthalmology, and otorhinolaryngology. The book comprehensively covers 52 categories of diseases, along with detailed information on formula composition, preparations, decoction techniques, application, contraindications, therapeutic principles and methods, medicinal compatibility within compound formulas, and treatment based on pattern identification. Its comprehensive coverage has significantly contributed to the formation of the "principle-method-formula-medicine" framework. The formulas in this book are mostly composed of one or two Chinese medicines, which indicates the embryonic stage of formula studies, and reflects the real situation of the transition from scattered records to systematic and specialized organization in this field.

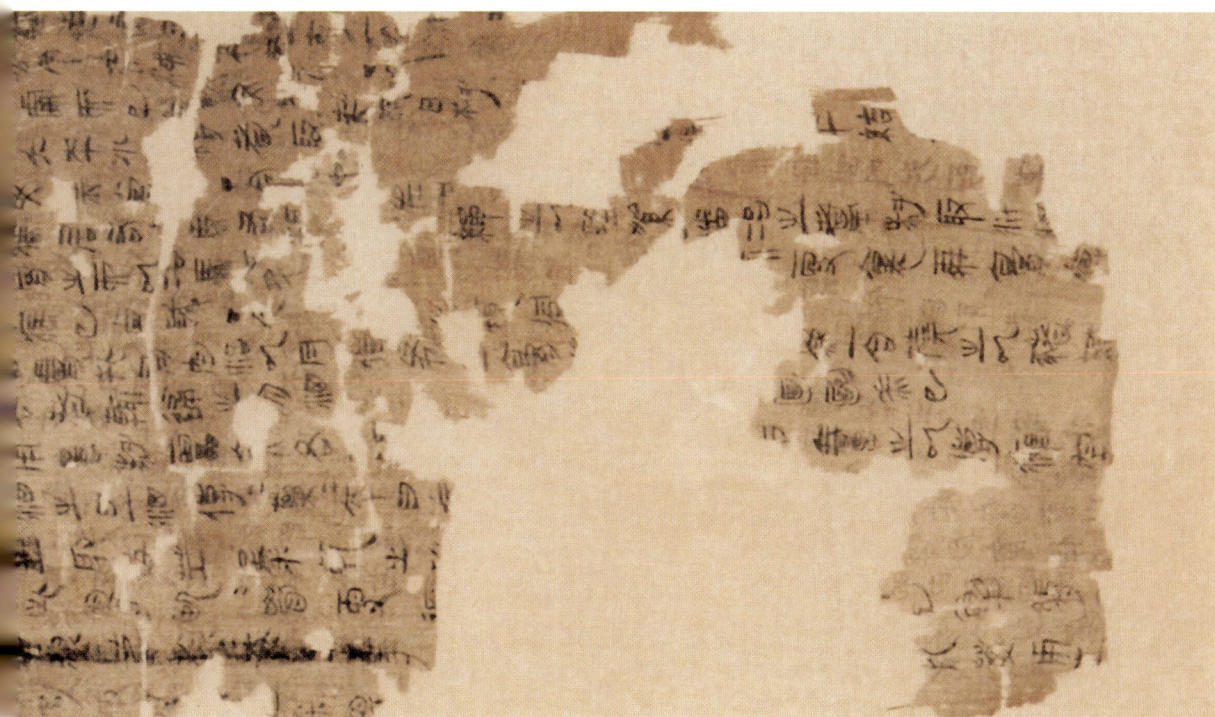

辨证论治是中医学的特色和精华所在，而马王堆医学已初步呈现辨证论治思想的思维迹象。比如，《五十二病方》关于药物的配伍规律，除增减药味来改变方剂的组成外，还采用了药量加减法，反映了先秦时期药物应用已从单味药发展成多味药的情况，体现了中医早期辨证论治、随症加减的特征。并且，此期方剂的应用不仅有对症治疗，还有自觉运用多味药组成复方的能力与实例。"同病异治"的辨治思想亦有体现，如《五十二病方》在疸病篇中，列出了治疸基础方，书云："睢（疸）病，冶白莶（蔹）、黄蓍（芪）、芍乐（药）、桂、姜、椒、朱（茱）臾（萸），凡七物……并以三指大最（撮）一入杯酒中，日五六饮之。"根据疸病不同类型，书中又提出"骨疸倍白蔹，肉疸倍黄芪，肾疸倍芍药，其余各一。"这表明，当时人们已经有了依据不同症状、疾病分型来辨证论治的早期辨治思想。有关经络辨证的内容在马王堆医书中亦有记载。《足臂十一脉灸经》完整论述了 11 条经脉的生理、病理及治疗方法，《阴阳十一脉灸经》记录了"是动病"与"所生病"的灸法治疗。

Treatment based on pattern identification is the characteristic and essence of CM, and Mawangdui medicine has initially presented some signs of it. For example, in terms of medicinal combination rules in the *Formulas for Fifty-two Diseases*, the composition of a formula can be modified by adding or subtracting not only the types of Chinese medicines but also the doses of them. It reflects the transformation from the single-medicine application to the multi-medicine one in the pre-Qin period, which exhibits the early features of treatment based on pattern identification and modifying formulas according to symptoms in CM. Moreover, it shows not only symptomatic treatment with formulas, but also the ability and examples to consciously use multiple medicines to form compound formulas in the period. At the same time, the idea of "different treatments for the same disease" is also reflected. For instance, the chapter of "Ju disease[4]" in the *Formulas for Fifty-two Diseases* records that the basic formula for treating this disease is composed of Bailian (Ampelopsis Radix), Huangqi(Astragali Radix), Shaoyao (Paeoniae Radix), Gui (Cinnamomi Cortex), Jiang (Zingiberis Rhizoma), Jiao (Zanthoxyli Pericarpium), and Zhuyu (Euodiae Fructus), and it is advised to take three fingertips (pinching) and put it into a cup of wine, and then drink it five or six times a day. According to the different types of Ju disease, it is also proposed that "double the dose of Bailian (Ampelopsis Radix) in bone Ju, double the dose of Huangqi(Astragali Radix) in flesh Ju, double the dose of Shaoyao(Paeoniae Radix) in kidney Ju, and keep the remaining medicines one dose". This shows that people at that time already developed the early concept of treating disease based on different symptoms and disease patterns. Furthermore, the contents related to pattern identification of meridians is also recorded in Mawangdui medical books. The *Moxibustion Classic of the Eleven Meridians of the Foot and Forearm* fully discusses the physiology, pathology, and treatment methods of 11 meridians, and the *Moxibustion Classic of the Eleven Yin-Yang Meridians* records the moxibustion treatment of "是动病(diseases caused by the dysfunction of qi in a certain meridian)" and "所生病(disease which can be treated by the acupoints of a certain meridian)".

---

[4] Ju disease is also known as deep-rooted ulcer. It is a collective term for ulcers in bones or joints due to exogenous pathogens or stagnation of qi and blood. It may develop into inward collapse of toxins or fistulas.

自 20 世纪 70 年代马王堆医书出土，中国乃至世界各地的学者对其掀起了研究和传播的热潮。虽然由于出土医书成书年代较早，加之部分内容存在残破、缺失的现象，使马王堆医学文化在表现形式上整体趋于零散、朴素，但是随着研究、整理和挖掘工作的深入、系统开展，目前已形成语言文字学、药物学、方剂学、养生学、经络针灸学等多个领域的代表性研究成果。时间医学、骨伤科、男科、胎产生殖理论、生命观、祝由疗法与巫祝文化等其他医论方面的研究，也处于百花齐放的状态。相信，未来马王堆医学文化一定会走向世界、福泽后世，绽放出东方健康智慧的光彩。

Since the discovery of medical books in the Mawangdui Han Dynasty Tombs in the 1970s, scholars in China and around the world have sparked a wave of research and disseminationin the past 50 years. Despite the fact that the unearthed medical books were written at a quite early time and some of the contents are missing, the overall expression of the Mawangdui medical culturet ends to be fragmented and simple as well, with the increasingly in-depth and systematic research, sorting, and excavation, representative research achievements have been seen in a variety of fields such as linguistics, Chinese medicines and formulas, health preservation, meridians, as well as acupuncture and moxibustion. In addition, research on chronomedicine, orthopedics and traumatology, andrology, obstetrics, reproductive health, outlook on life, Zhuyou therapy, and witchcraft culture, among other medical theories, is also in a state of flourishing. It is believed that in the future, the Mawangdui medical culture, blooming with the radiance of Oriental wisdom on health, will transcend ancient and modern times, step toward the world, and ultimately benefit future generations.

经脉学说里的

传世医道

The Inherited Medical Principles in
Meridian Theory

# 马王堆

经络与针砭医术是中国传统医学的核心组成部分，伴随着中华文化的形成和发展，为华夏人民的健康维系和繁衍生息做出了极其重要的贡献。经络学说建立在砭、针、灸等疗法的丰富经验和身体各部"气穴"与内脏相联系的概念的基础之上，并结合了当时解剖学的成就而创立，对奠定针灸疗法的理论基础具有重大的指导意义。马王堆汉墓出土医书《足臂十一脉灸经》《阴阳十一脉灸经》是迄今发现的最古老的经络学著作，而《脉法》《阴阳脉死候》提出了最早的脉学理论。这些出土医书构成了研究中医经络学说起源的珍贵资料，为溯源后世的经络学说，以及针灸砭术等医学技术的形成和发展奠定了重要的基础。

Meridians and needling therapy are pivotal components of CM. Accompanying the formation and development of Chinese culture, they have made extremely important contributions to the health maintenance and reproduction of the Chinese people. The meridian theory was formulated on the foundation of extensive practical experience with stone needling, acupuncture, moxibustion, and various other therapies, as well as the idea that "qi points" located in different body parts are connected to corresponding internal organs. Besides, it incorporated the anatomical knowledge of the time. Consequently, it has played a significant guiding role in laying the theoretical basis for acupuncture and moxibustion. The *Moxibustion Classic of the Eleven Meridians of the Foot and Forearm* and the *Moxibustion Classic of the Eleven Yin-Yang Meridians* unearthed from the Mawangdui Han Dynasty Tombs have been the earliest discovered works on meridians. Similarly, the *Treatment Methods based on Meridians* and the *Death Signs of Yin-Yang Meridians* have proposed the earliest pulse theory. These medical books are valuable materials for studying the origin of the meridian theory, and have set an important stage for the formation and development of the meridian theory, as well as the medical techniques of needling therapy in the later generations.

《足臂十一脉灸经》全文共 34 行，1000 余字。出土时与《阴阳十一脉灸经》甲本，以及《脉法》《阴阳脉死候》《五十二病方》同抄在一幅长帛上。该医书用篆意较浓的古隶抄写，没有标题，但文中"足""臂"二字高出正文一格书写，可知此篇可分为"足"脉和"臂"脉两部分。书中以"足"表示下肢脉，共有 6 条；以"臂"表示上肢脉，共有 5 条。这 11 条脉的排列原则是先足后手，循行的基本规律是从四肢末端到胸腹或头面部。与现行的经脉学理论不同的是，《足臂十一脉灸经》只记录有 11 条经脉，并且其循行方向都是向心性的，每一条脉下简要叙述了其循行部位、所主病候和灸法。但是，其病候描述简单而原始，如手太阳、手阳明、手少阴三脉，每脉仅举 1 病，多者如足少阳脉主 16 病，足太阳脉主 15 病。《足臂十一脉灸经》论及各经脉所主疾病共计 78 种，尚未对疾病进行分类。并且诸脉没有理论和治则上的阐述，仅足厥阴脉后面有一些关于病候预后的记述。治疗方法全是灸法，只说灸某脉，没有穴位名称，更没有针治记载。由此观之，《足臂十一脉灸经》是最早的经脉学著作，可认定为中医经络学说形成的雏形，为论证针灸治疗学发展史上针灸流派形成的时间问题等提供了史实依据。

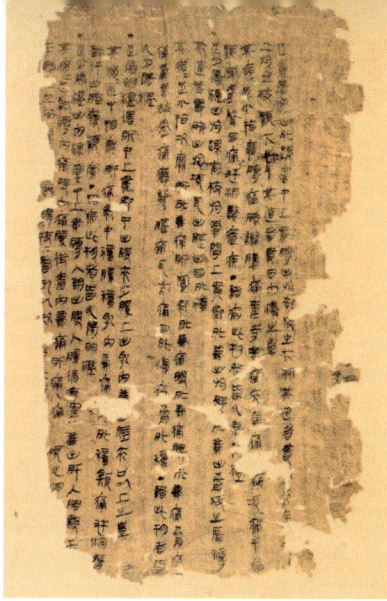

马王堆三号墓出土帛书《足臂十一脉灸经》（局部图）
Silk Manuscript of the *Moxibustion Classic of the Eleven Meridians of the Foot and Forearm* in Tomb 3 (Partial Picture)

The full text of the *Moxibustion Classic of the Eleven Meridians of the Foot and Forearm* consists of 34 lines and more than 1,000 Chinese characters. When unearthed, it appeared on a long piece of silk along with the version A of the *Moxibustion Classic of the Eleven Yin-Yang Meridians*, the *Treatment Methods based on Meridians*, the *Death Signs of Yin-Yang Meridians*, and the *Formulas for Fifty-two Diseases*. The text is transcribed in the old clerical script, an ancient form of calligraphy prevalent during the Qin Dynasty (221—207 B.C.), retaining the distinct style of the seal script. It has no title, but the character writing of "足(foot)"and "臂(arm)" are written one grid higher than the remaining-characters, indicating that this medical book can be divided into two sections, i.e., foot meridians and arm meridians. In the book, "足(foot)" represents the meridians of the lower limbs, totaling six, while "臂(arm)"the meridians of the upper limbs, totaling five. The meridians of the lower limbs are arranged prior to those of the upper ones, and the basic rule of their course is from the ends of the four limbs to the chest, abdomen, or head and face. Unlike the current theory of meridians, this book records only 11 meridians, and the direction of their pathways is considered to be centripetal. The pathway, indications, and moxibustion method of each meridian are briefly described. However, the description of the indications is simple and primitive. For example, the indications of the three meridians of hand-Taiyang, hand-Yangming, and hand-Shaoyin are illustrated by only one disease respectively, whereas most of the indications are listed in the foot-Shaoyang meridian with 16 diseases and the foot-Taiyang meridian with 15 diseases. The book discusses a total of 78 diseases related to the meridians, but no classification is made for these diseases. And there is no explanation for the theory or therapeutic principles of those meridians, only a discussion about the prognosis of the indications recorded in the section of the foot-Jueyin meridian. The only recorded treatment method is moxibustion, simply referring to moxibustion on a certain meridian without any name of the acupoint involved and any record of acupuncture. From this point of view, the *Moxibustion Classic of the Eleven Meridians of the Foot and Forearm*, as the earliest work on the meridians, can be identified as the prototype of CM meridian theory. It provides a historical basis for demonstrating the time of the formation of various schools in the development history of acupuncture and moxibustion therapeutics.

　　《阴阳十一脉灸经》因发掘出同一内容的两种写本，故有甲本和乙本之分。甲本共 37 行，现存 583 字，和《足臂十一脉灸经》等同抄在一幅长帛上；而乙本则抄录在另一帛幅上，首尾较完整，但中间缺文较多，共 18 行，现存 793 字。因此，甲、乙两本二者可相互弥补而基本保持了该医书的完整性。《阴阳十一脉灸经》全书分为"阳"（代表阳经经脉）与"阴"（代表阴经经脉）两篇。11 脉排列次序是阳脉在前，阴脉在后。全身经脉（除肩脉与足少阴脉以外）由四肢走向躯体中心，肩脉与足少阴脉由头或少腹走向四肢末端。该书论述的内容较《足臂十一脉灸经》有了较大的进步和丰富，它在《足臂十一脉灸经》的基础上，对人体 11 条经脉的循行路径、生理病理做了调整和补充，被认为是我国最早的灸疗学专著。其经脉循行方向开始出现远心循行，各脉主治疾病较《足臂十一脉灸经》更详细和完善，所主病从前者的 78 种病增加到 147 种病。《阴阳十一脉灸经》和《灵枢·经脉》从内容到词句有许多相同之处，说明它们之间存在某种学术脉络关系。《阴阳十一脉灸经》成书年代较《黄帝内经》更早，故可以说其为《黄帝内经》经脉学说的形成奠定了基础。

马王堆三号墓出土帛书《阴阳十一脉灸经》（甲本）、《脉法》、《阴阳脉死候》（局部图）

Silk Manuscripts of the *Moxibustion Classic of the Eleven Yin-Yang Meridians* (Version A), *the Treatment Methods based on Meridians, and the Death Signs of Yin-Yang Meridians* in Tomb 3 (Partial Picture)

马王堆三号墓出土帛书《阴阳十一脉灸经》（乙本局部图）
Silk Manuscript of the *Moxibustion Classic of the Eleven Yin-Yang Meridians* (Version B) in Tomb 3 (Partial Picture)

The *Moxibustion Classic of the Eleven Yin-Yang Meridians* has two versions due to the discovery of two manuscripts of the same contents. Version A consists of 37 lines with 583 characters extant, which is transcribed on a long silk piece along with the *Moxibustion Classic of the Eleven Meridians of the Foot and Forearm*. Version B is on another piece of silk, with a relatively complete beginning and end but a lot of missing text in the middle, totaling 18 lines and 793 characters extant. The two versions basically maintain the integrity of the book and can complement each other.The full text of the book has two parts: "Yang" (representing the yang meridians) and "Yin" (representing the yin meridians). The yang meridians are arranged prior to the yin meridians. It describes that the meridians of the whole body run from the limbs to the center of the body, except for the shoulder and foot-Shaoyin meridians, which run reversely from the head or lateral lower abdomen to the extremities. The contents discussed in this book are more improved and plentiful than those in the *Moxibustion Classic of the Eleven Meridians of the Foot and Forearm*. It adjusts and supplements the pathways, physiological functions, and pathological changes of the 11 meridians based on the *Moxibustion Classic of the Eleven Meridians of the Foot and Forearm* and has been considered as the earliest treatise on moxibustion in China. For instance, the distal running of the meridians firstly appears in this book, and the indications of each meridian are more detailed and comprehensive than those in the *Moxibustion Classic of the Eleven Meridians of the Foot and Forearm*, the total number of which increases from 78 in the latter book to 147. Moreover, the *Moxibustion Classic of the Eleven Yin-Yang Meridians* and the chapter of "Meridians" in the *Spiritual Pivot* have many similarities in both contents and wording, indicating a certain academic connection between them. Being written earlier, the *Moxibustion Classic of the Eleven Yin-Yang Meridians* has laid the foundation for the formation of the meridian theory in the *Huangdi's Classic of Medicine*.

《脉法》是目前发现的先秦时期唯一一部民间医学教材，在帛书上位于《足臂十一脉灸经》《阴阳十一脉灸经》之后，内容是简明扼要地向学生传授有关导脉、启脉、相脉的重要原则和方法。由于历时久远，《脉法》文字损毁太多，只能辨认出全文的一半。幸运的是，1974年在湖北江陵张家山汉墓出土了一批简牍书，其中的《脉书》有一段文字与《脉法》基本相同。将简牍相应的字补入帛书后，虽然还有十余字阙如，但《脉法》内容已经大致明了。校对补充之后的《脉法》原文一共13行，430余字。所谓"导脉"，即通过灸法、砭法疏通引导脉气；而"启脉"即用砭石刺脉放血治疗痈脓；"相脉"关乎具体的诊脉方法，提及六种脉象，并论述了诊脉的脉名及要求。《脉法》不仅揭示了古代医家对脉的基本认识，还提出一套基本完整的砭灸诊疗方法。其突出的学术价值在于，最早提出并确立了人体气与脉之间的联系，初步揭示了气在经脉中的传导及脉气作用于人体的生理规律。同时，《脉法》还提出了"故圣人寒头而煖（暖）足"的养生理念和原则，最早确立了治病"取有余而益不足"的虚实补泻的概念，对治病的总原则进行了论述。这些思想后面也一直贯穿《黄帝内经》等古典医籍之中，由此可见，《脉法》中蕴含的古朴医学思想影响了后世医家对治病原则的认识，推动着中医学的发展与进步，反之也有助于后来人对中医史追本溯源的研究。

The *Treatment Methods based on Meridians* is the only currently discovered folk medical textbook in the pre-Qin period. Placed after the *Moxibustion Classic of the Eleven Meridians of the Foot and Forearm* and the *Moxibustion Classic of the Eleven Yin-Yang Meridians* on the same silk piece, it concisely instructs students in important principles and methods related to guiding meridian, meridian bloodletting, and pulse-taking. Due to its long history, the book has been damaged too much, and only half of the entire text can be recognized. Fortunately, in 1974, a batch of bamboo slips were unearthed from the Zhangjiashan Han Dynasty Tombs in Jiangling, Hubei Province. Among them, the *Book of Meridians* contains a passage that is basically identical to the one discovered in the *Treatment Methods based on Meridians*. Hence, despite over 10 missing characters, by incorporating the corresponding characters from the bamboo slips into the silk books, the contents of the *Treatment Methods based on Meridians* have been roughly understood. After undergoing proofreading and supplementation, its text consists of 13 lines and approximately 430 characters. In this book, "导脉 (guiding meridian)" refers to unblocking and guiding the meridian qi through moxibustion and stone needling. "启脉 (meridian bloodletting)" outlines the principle of treating abscesses by meridian bloodletting with stone needles. Lastly, "相脉 (pulse-taking)" deals with specific pulse diagnosis methods, mentioning six distinct pulse manifestations and discussing various pulse names along with the prerequisites for accurate pulse-taking. The *Treatment Methods based on Meridians* not only reveals the basic understanding of meridians by ancient medical practitioners, but also proposes a basically complete set of diagnosis and treatment methods of stone needling and moxibustion. Its outstanding academic value lies in that it has been the first to establish the connection between the human body's qi and meridians, preliminarily revealing the qi transmission in the meridians and the physiological laws of the action of meridian qi on the body. Moreover, the book also put forwards the health preservation idea and principle of "keeping the head cold and the feet warm". Additionally, when discussing the general treatment principles, it has been the first to introduce the concept of "reducing the excess while supplementing the deficiency". These ideas have been echoed in subsequent medical classics as well, such as the *Spiritual Pivot* and the *Basic Questions*. Thus, it is evident that the primitive medical ideas encompassed in the *Treatment Methods based on Meridians* have shaped the comprehension of treatment principles among subsequent medical practitioners, driving the advancement and evolution of CM and facilitating origin research for future generations.

在马王堆汉墓出土医书中，除上述 3 种之外，同抄于一幅帛书上的《阴阳脉死候》和《五十二病方》同样载有与经脉、灸法及砭法相关的内容。《阴阳脉死候》总共只有 4 行，全文 100 余字，主要对三阴脉、三阳脉病的死候做了原则性的概括和提示。《五十二病方》作为最古老的医方著作，书中除药剂外，记录的治疗方法还包括灸法、砭法，但没有针法。涉及的病症包括阴囊及睾丸肿痛、小便不通、毒蛇咬伤、肛门痒痛、痔核、疣病、痂病等。

Among the medical books unearthed from the Mawangdui Han Dynasty Tombs, there are several volumes pertaining to meridians, acupuncture, moxibustion, and stone needling. Apart from the three books mentioned above, two other notable texts are the *Death Signs of Yin-Yang Meridians* and the *Formulas for Fifty-two Diseases*, both transcribed on the same long piece of silk. The *Death Signs of Yin-Yang Meridians* contains only four lines and over 100 characters, mainly summarizing the death signs of diseases related to the three yin meridians and three yang meridians. The oldest medical book on formulas, the *Formulas for Fifty-two Diseases*, documents not just medications, but also therapeutic methods like moxibustion and stone needling. Unfortunately, acupuncture is not included in the book. The range of diseases addressed in it spans from swelling and pain in the scrotum and testicles, difficulty in urination, snake bites, anal itching and pain, hemorrhoids, warts, to Ju disease and many others.

经络与针砭医术一直是中医学独特的医学技术，以其对人体独到的认知，独特的治疗理念、方法和显著的临床疗效著称于世，享誉海内外。作为"一带一路"倡议的一张闪亮名片，中医学"出海"之路越走越宽，目前已传播至 196 个国家和地区。根据世界卫生组织统计，目前已有 113 个会员国认可使用针灸，其中 29 个设立了传统医学的法律法规，20 个将针灸纳入医疗保险体系。马王堆医学文化蕴藏着丰富的经络学理论知识及针砭医术的实践经验，在中医学发展长河中占据重要的地位。深入挖掘、创新转化这些古代医籍中的宝贵经验，让马王堆医学文化活起来、走出去，会为人类健康福祉做出更大的贡献。

Meridians and needling therapies have always been unique medical techniques of traditional of CM, both domestically and internationally renowned for its unique comprehension of the human body, distinctive treatment ideologies and practices, as well as its impressive clinical effectiveness. As a shining business card of the Belt and Road Initiative, CM has now reached 196 countries and regions. According to statistics from WHO, 113 member countries have approved the use of acupuncture, 29 of which have established laws and regulations on traditional medicine, and another 20 have integrated acupuncture into their medical insurance system. The Mawangdui medical culture contains rich theoretical knowledge of meridians and practical experience in needling therapy, occupying a significant position in the development of CM. It is time to revitalize and globalize the Mawangdui medical culture by deeply exploring, continuously innovating and scientifically transforming the valuable experiences in these ancient medical books, which will make even greater contributions to human health and well-being.

生命讯息

《导引图》流转的

# The Life Messages Conveyed in the
## *Drawings of Guiding and Stretching*

导引作为一种强身健体、防病致病的功法，在中国有着悠久的历史。据宋代罗泌《路·史前记》记载，在上古"阴康氏"时代，由于水路失于疏泄，先民长期生活在潮湿恶劣的自然环境当中，湿寒阴气凝于体内，因此得了一种筋骨萎缩、腿脚发肿、活动不灵的疾病。于是，有人便创造了一种类似舞蹈的锻炼身体的方法，"教人以引舞以导之"，这便是后来"导引"的由来。春秋战国时期，导引养生开始盛行，先秦时期诸子百家思想也深刻影响着导引养生观。马王堆三号墓出土的帛图——《导引图》，真实地反映了2200 余年前中国古人通过导引运动谐调形神、防治疾病的生动情景，给人们提供了有关导引疗法极为重要的实物资料。

马王堆三号墓出土帛图《导引图》
Silk Painting of the *Drawings of Guiding and Stretching* in Tomb 3

Daoyin (guiding and stretching exercise), as an exercise for body building and disease prevention and treatment, has a long history in China. According to the preface of the *Unofficial History* by Luo Mi in the Song Dynasty (960—1279), as early as the ancient times of "Yinkang", due to the lack of drainage in waterways, Chinese ancestors lived in a damp and harsh natural environment for a long time. Consequently, with the accumulation of dampness and cold in the body, people suffered from a disease manifested as muscle and tendon atrophy, swelling of legs and feet, and lack of mobility. A set of physical exercise similar to dance was then created to "teach people to stretch the body and guide the flow of qi". This is the origin of "daoyin". During the periods of Spring and Autumn and Warring States (770—221 B.C.), preserving health by daoyin began to prevail. Meanwhile, the view of preserving health by daoyin was profoundly influenced by various schools of thought during the pre-Qin period. The painting on silk, the *Drawings of Guiding and Stretching* unearthed from Tomb 3, truly portrays the vivid scenes of ancient Chinese people using daoyin to harmonize their body and spirits as well as to prevent and treat diseases over 2,200 years ago. This artwork provides an invaluable material reference for understanding daoyin therapy.

经过复原后发现，《导引图》高约 50 厘米、长约 100 厘米，图中彩绘有 44 个不同运动姿态的图像，分别绘成上下 4 层。人像高 9 厘米到 12 厘米，有男有女，有老有少。这些人物都以工笔彩绘，用黑色线条勾画轮廓，然后填以朱红或青灰带蓝色彩，除少数人像手持器物以外，所有人像都是徒手运动的。从《导引图》所绘的人像及其所着服饰来看，人像多为庶民阶层。他们的头发或整齐盘起或戴着便帽，脚上穿着尖角形鞋履或赤足。其中多数人身着褶袴式的无絮短袍，有的着裙襦式衣裳（即单层的连衣连裙式服装），有的穿短裤短裙，还有少数几位赤裸着上身，这些与四川成都凤凰山出土汉代画像砖中收割的农民服饰基本相同。更能吸引我们的是他们丰富、生动、活跃的体态，44 种姿态、44 个动作串连成一片行云流水的世界，在时光斑驳的画卷中舒展流转，传递着神秘的生命讯息。

After restoration, it is found that the *Drawings of Guiding and Stretching* is about 50 centimeters high and 100 centimeters long. In it 44 figures with different motion postures painted in color, arranged into four rows. Men or women, old or young, the figures are about 9—12 centimeters tall. They are all meticulously painted, contoured with black lines, and then colored in vermilion or steel gray. Except for a few holding objects, all figures are bare-handed. It can be inferred from the figures and their costumes that most of them are the common people, neatly coiling up their hair or putting on caps, and wearing pointed shoes or being barefoot. Most of them are dressed in pleated short robes, single-layer dresses, or short pants and skirts, and there are a few whose upper body are bare, the clothing of which is basically the same as that of the harvesting farmers in the brick reliefs of the Han Dynasty unearthed in Fenghuang Mountain, Chengdu, Sichuan Province. What attracts peoples more is that these 44 postures, or in other words, 44 motions, various, vivid, and active, are connected naturally and smoothly to form a river of life, flowing freely in the fuzzy painting of time and conveying mysterious life messages constantly.

马王堆三号墓出土帛图《导引图》的
复原图
Restored Image of the *Drawings of Guiding and Stretching* on Silk in Tomb 3

　　"导引"一词最早见于《庄子·刻意》，书曰："吹呴呼吸，吐故纳新，熊经鸟申，为寿而已矣。此导引之士，养形之人，彭祖寿考者之所好也。"这里对导引的具体描述即"状如熊之攀枝，鸟之伸脚"，通过模仿熊、鸟的活动形态来伸展肢体，调和气血，达到健康长寿的目的。对"导引"的解释，古籍中有不同的记载，有的解释为呼吸运动，有的解释为肢体运动，有的则认为导引包括呼吸运动和肢体运动。从马王堆《导引图》来看，画中不光有模仿"熊经""鸟伸"等动物形象，还有其他类型的肢体运动和多种呼吸运动，还有些人像在做瞑目存想状。所谓瞑目存想，即集中意念来感受、对话自己身体的某一个部位，感受大自然的某种美好景象，从而使自己心情舒畅，古人认为，通过瞑目存想可以治疗疾病。综合上述各种说法，我们一般认为"导引"是呼吸运动、肢体运动和意念活动三者相结合的一种宣导气血、引治疾病的保健功。

The term "daoyin" firstly appears in the chapter of "Culture" in the book of *ZhuangZi*, which says, "Breathe in and out slowly and steadily to exhale the waste gas and inhale the fresh air, exercise like bear climbing tree and bird stretching legs, so as to prolong life-span. These are favorite practices of those who are good at daoyin and health preservation, such as the legendary figure Peng Zu, known for his exceptional longevity." This is a specific description for daoyin, in which, by imitating the movements of bears and birds to stretch the body and harmonize qi and blood, the goal of health and longevity is to be achieved. There are various interpretations of "daoyin" in ancient books, some interpreting it as breathing exercise, others as bodily exercise, and still others as the combination of both. From the *Drawings of Guiding and Stretching* of Mawangdui, it can be seen that the figures not only imitate animal motions such as "bear climbing" and "bird stretching", but also exhibit other types of bodily exercise and various breathing exercise. Moreover, some figures appear to be meditating with their eyes closed. The so-called "meditation with eyes closed" refers to concentrating the mind to feel and converse with a certain part of the body or imagine a beautiful natural scenery, aiming to make the exerciser feel comfortable and treat illnesses. Based on the various statements mentioned above, it is generally believe now that daoyin is a kind of healthcare exercises that combines breathing and bodily exercises, as well as the regulation of mental activity to promote qi and blood circulation and treat illnesses.

从导引功法的具体形式来看，马王堆出土的《导引图》主要包括四个方面的功法内容：一是徒手运动，帛画中大部分都为徒手运动，包括伸展、屈膝、侧体、转体、跳跃等。二是器械操作，譬如"以杖通阴阳"，即描绘了一个穿裙妇女借助长棒，伸展拉伸躯体以"调和阴阳"的功法。帛图中还出现了盘、棍、球、袋四种器械，用来辅助行功。三是行气吐纳，譬如仰呼，帛图中绘一男子直立，挺胸，两臂举向后上方，作仰天长啸的姿态。四是意念活动，某些图像表现为凝神入静的存想状态。而从术式的功能来看，可以进一步分为养生功和医疗功。养生功是主要以养生保健为目的，模仿各种动物动作的功法（如螳螂、龙登、熊经、鹞背、猿猴等仿生功法）。譬如"螳螂功法"，保持两足并立，两手上举，延伸至极限（自己感到的极限），然后转腰向左右弯曲。医疗功主要以治疗为目的，或作为辅助治疗手段，促使机体恢复健康，表述为标明"引"治某种疾病的术式，如引颓、引温病、引膝痛等。譬如"引颓"，颓即颓疝之病，现代称腹股沟斜疝，保持两足左右分开与肩同宽，站立，两膝关节微向前屈，双手微外展并且下垂，头部向前微俯。

《导引图》之器械操作类功法——以杖通阴阳
"Using a Rod to Connect Yin and Yang", an Exercise with Equipment in the *Drawings of Guiding and Stretching*

《导引图》之行气吐纳类功法——仰呼
"Exhaling with Head Raised", a Breathing Exercise in the *Drawings of Guiding and Stretching*

From the specific forms of daoyin in the *Drawings of Guiding and Stretching*, four aspects of the exercises in daoyin are mainly illustrated. The first aspect is bare-handed exercises. Most of the motions depicted in the painting on silk are of this type, including stretching, knee bending, lateral bending, twisting, jumping, etc. The second is the ones with equipment. For example, a woman wearing a skirt in the painting uses a rod to stretch her body in order to "harmonize yin and yang", which is named "using a rod to connect yin and yang". Four additional types of equipment, including discs, sticks, balls, and bags, are used to assist in exercise. The third is breathing exercises. For instance, a man in the painting stands upright, with his chest out and his arms raised backwards and upwards, in a posture of shouting towards the sky, which is known as "exhaling with head raised". The fourth is the regulation of mental activity, as some figures show a state of meditation. From the perspective of function, daoyin can be classified into health-preserving exercises and therapeutic exercises. Health-preserving exercises are mainly for the purpose of health care by imitating movements of various animals such as mantis, dragon, bear, sparrow hawk, monkey. For example, the practice of the "Mantis Technique" is: keep two feet standing side by side, raise both arms and stretch them to the limit, and then turn the waist to bend left and right. Therapeutic exercises mainly aim at treating illnesses or serving as an auxiliary therapeutic means to promote the body to restore health. Those techniques attributed to this type are labeled as "引(treating)", i.e., to treat a certain disease in the *Drawings*, such as "引頽 (treating tui)", "treating warm diseases", and "treating knee pain". Taking "引頽 (treating tui)"as an example, in which "頽(tui) "means a kind of hernia which is known as indirect inguinal hernia in modern medicine, it involves standing with feet apart at shoulder width, knees slightly bent forward, hands down and palms slightly facing forward, and head slightly leaning forward.

《导引图》之养生功——螳螂功法
"Mantis Technique", a Health-Preserving Exercise in the *Drawings of Guiding and Stretching*

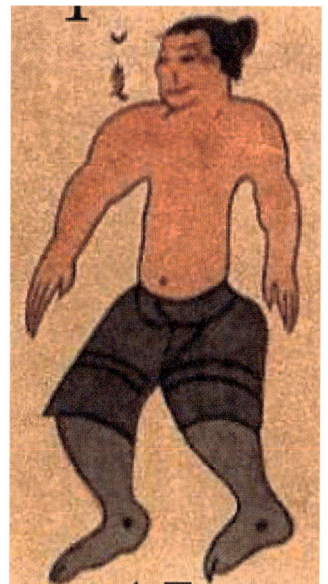

《导引图》之医疗功——引頽
"Yin Tui (Treating Tui)", a Therapeutic Exercise in the *Drawings of Guiding and Stretching*

中国古代医家和养生学家结合防病治病实践，对导引的功能有着丰富的认识。现代中医学认为，导引的作用是通过各种练功手段进行锻炼和活动，从而加强人体的气化作用来实现的。导引作为一种健身运动，可以对机体起到平衡阴阳、调和气血、疏通经络、培植真气、强筋壮骨的作用。根据人体阴阳盛衰情况，可施以对应的导引运动形式和手段，若阳气旺盛则以静式为主，若阴气旺盛则以动式为主，从而动静结合、外动内静、动中求静，达到"动静互根，阴阳平秘"的状态。同时，导引还能通过肢体运动和呼吸吐纳等手段，促进人体气血交换，激发"经络之气"，疏通或强化经脉，使气血趋于顺畅调和。因此，导引的许多功法都有调呼吸、促消化、培育真气的作用，古代更有"内练精、气、神，外练筋、骨、皮"的说法。

Ancient Chinese doctors and health-preserving experts, combined with the practice of disease prevention and treatment, had rich knowledge on the function of daoyin. Modern Chinese medicine believes that the role of daoyin is to be achieved by strengthening qi transformation in the body through various exercises. As a fitness exercise, daoyin balances yin and yang, harmonizes qi and blood, unblocks meridians, cultivates primordial qi, and strengthens tendons and bones in the body. Based on the condition of yin and yang, daoyin adopts corresponding forms and methods. For example, the static exercises (which actually display static exterior and dynamic interior) are mainly applied if yang is exuberant, and the dynamic exercises (which actually act as dynamic exterior and static interior, seeking calmness from movements) are applied if yin is predominant, through which, movement and stillness are combined, achieving a state of "mutual dependence between movement and stillness, and balance between yin and yang". At the same time,by physical movements and breathing exercises, daoyin also promotes the inter-transformation of qi and blood in the body, stimulates the meridian qi, unblocks or strengthens the meridians, and makes the circulation of qi and blood tend to be smooth and harmonious. Therefore, many techniques of daoyin have the functions of regulating respiration, promoting digestion, and cultivating primordial qi. Furthermore, in ancient times, there was a saying that daoyin "cultivates essence, qi, and spiritinternally, and strengthens tendons, bones, and skin externally".

马王堆导引术开创了中国导引运动养生之先河，在其后的两千多年历史中，它不仅一直被医家和养生学家广泛采用，还被道教和佛教广泛用作修炼身心之法。医圣华佗采撷《导引图》之精华，创造了"五禽戏"，"五禽戏"不仅使他自身"年且百岁，尤有壮容"，更是流传至今，成为中国传统保健体育代表项目。后世以马王堆《导引图》功法为蓝本，整理出一套"马王堆导引健身功"。此导引法除预备式和收势外，具体功法包括 12 势，以循经导引、行意相随为主要特点，达到形、气、神一体的练功境界。动作围绕肢体开合提落、旋转屈伸、押筋拔骨进行设计，动作优美，衔接流畅，安全可靠，简单易学，适合不同人群习练，具有祛病强身、延年益寿的功效。马王堆《导引图》作为现存最早的一卷保健运动的工笔彩绘帛画，为古代文献中失散不全的多种导引与健身运动找到了最早的图谱资料，也为研究导引的历史发展提供了研究线索，对我国运动养生文化的发展具有极其重要的价值。

The Mawangdui Daoyin Techniques pioneers the sports regimen in China. In the following two thousand years, it has not only been widely adopted by doctors and health-preserving experts, but also continuously used as a method for cultivating the body and mind in Taoism and Buddhism. The medical sage Hua Tuo created the five-animal exercises by adopting the essence of the *Drawings of Guiding and Stretching*, which made him "almost a hundred years old, but still look strong". Moreover, the five-animal exercises has been handed down, becoming a representative of traditional Chineses portsfor health maintenance.Besides, the later generations have compiled a set of "Mawangdui Daoyin Fitness Exercises"based on the techniques in the *Drawings of Guiding and Stretching*. In addition to the preparatory motion and the ending motion, this set of exercises includes 12 specific motions, mainly characterized by guiding the flow of it and stretching the body following the pathways of meridians, and synchronizing movements with mind, thus achieving a state where the body, qi, and spirit are integrated. The design of the movements focus on the limb's opening and closing, up and down, rotating, extending and flexing, as well as stretching of the tendons and bones. The movements are graceful, smoothly connected, safe and reliable, simple and easy to learn, suitable for different groups of people to practice, and have the effects of treating illnesses, strengthening the body, and prolonging life-span.As the earliest meticulous colored silk painting of health exercise extant, the *Drawings of Guiding and Stretching* unearthed from the Mawangdui Han Dynasty Tombs provides the earliest picture reference for a variety of scattered and incomplete daoyin and fitness exercises recorded in ancient documents. It also supplies research clues to studying the historical development of daoyin, and is extremely valuable for the development of sports regimen culture in China.

氤氲药香里的

# 防病锦囊

**The Disease Prevention Sachet with Misty Herbal Fragrance**

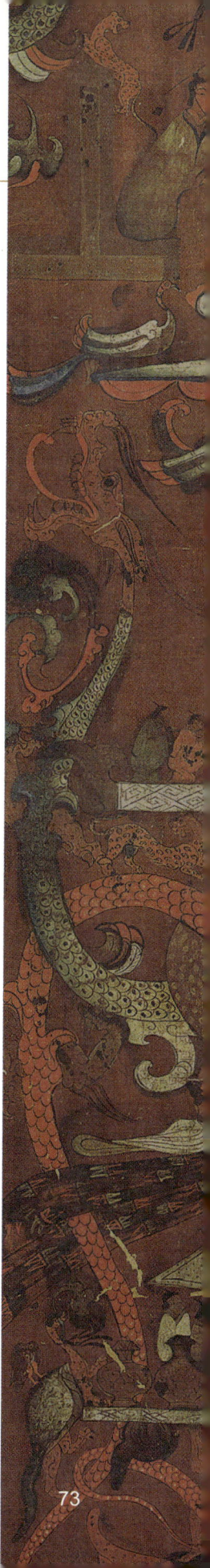

当被称为"东方睡美人"的辛追夫人首先展现在世人面前时，她的双手握着绣花绢面香囊，香囊内盛放着中草药。虽然这些中草药出土后碳化成了粉末，但是经过药学专家的专业鉴定，从中发现了茅香、高良姜、桂皮、杜衡、佩兰、花椒、辛夷、干姜、藁本9种药材。它们大多是含有挥发油的芳香类药物，可以起到抑菌防腐的作用。马王堆一号汉墓共出土了6个香囊，包括2个短款和4个长款，遣策上记载其为"熏囊"。短的香囊用于随身携带，长的香囊则挂于内室帷帐之间，反映了楚地"昼配香囊，夜用香枕"的习俗。一号墓边箱中的355号竹笥内的6个绢药袋中也装着香料草药，如辛夷、茅香、桂皮、花椒、干姜、杜衡、藁本、高良姜等。这些药物具有温阳通痹、温经通脉的作用，常用于治疗心腹冷痛、心痛、胁痛、寒痹等。它们出现在随葬品中并非偶然，很有可能与墓主人生前的生活习惯密切相关，这也成为辛追夫人主要死于冠心病的一个旁证。

马王堆一号墓出土的绢地"信期绣"香囊
Silk Sachet with "Xinqi Embroidery" in Tomb 1 ▶

▼ 马王堆一号墓出土的黄褐色对鸟菱纹绮地"信期绣"香囊
Ochre–Colored Paired Birds–Rhombus Patterned Brocade Sachet with "Xinqi Embroidery" in Tomb 1

马王堆一号墓出土的黄褐
色菱纹罗地"信期绣"
香囊
Ochre-Colored Rhombus Patterned Chiffon Sachet with
"Xinqi Embroidery" in Tomb 1

马王堆一号墓出土的黄褐
色菱纹罗地香囊
Ochre-Colored Rhombus Patterned Chiffon Sachet in Tomb 1

When Xin Zhui, known as the Lady of Dai and nicknamed the "Sleeping Beauty of the Orient", made her debut before the world, she gracefully clasped in her hand a sachet adorned with an embroidered silk cover and filled with a variety of herbs. Although these Chinese herbal medicines were carbonized into powder after excavation, nine herbs were found after professional identification by pharmaceutical experts, including Maoxiang (Hierochloe Odorata), Gaoliangjiang (Rhizoma Alpiniae Officinarum), Guipi (Cinnamomum Tamala), Duheng (Asarum Forbesii Maxim), Peilan (Herba Eupatorii), Huajiao (Pericarpium Zanthoxyli), Xinyi (Flos Magnoliae), Ganjiang (Zingiberis Rhizoma), and Gaoben (Rhizoma Ligustici). Most of them were aromatic drugs containing volatile oils that possess antibacterial and preservative properties. A total of six sachets, including two short-size and four long-size ones, were excavated from Mawangdui Han Dynasty Tomb 1. They were recorded as "fumigation sachets" by the list of funeral objects. The short-size sachets were intended for carrying around, whereas the long-size ones were hung between the curtains in the bedroom, reflecting the custom of "pairing sachets during the day and using aromatic pillow at night" in the Chu region. In the chamber next to Tomb 1, there were six silk bags containing spices and herbs, such as Xinyi (Flos Magnoliae), Maoxiang (Hierochloe Odorata), Guipi (Cinnamomum Tamala), Huajiao (Pericarpium Zanthoxyli), Ganjiang (Zingiberis Rhizoma), Duheng (Asarum Forbesii Maxim), Gaoben (Rhizoma Ligustici), and Gaoliangjiang (Rhizoma Alpiniae Officinarum). These drugs, which warm yang and meridians to promote blood circulation, are frequently utilized to treat cold pain in the chest and abdomen, chest pain, or cold impedement. Give their strong correlation with the lifestyle habits of the tomb owner during her lifetime, they offer collateral evidence suggesting that Xin Zhui primarily succumbed to coronary heart disease.

    香囊具有避邪除秽、驱除蚊虫等功用，中国古人佩戴香囊的历史可以追溯到先秦时代。位于长江流域的楚地，崇山峻岭，雨水充沛，植被丰富，是香料植物的主要产地，当地人对香料植物的运用更是炉火纯青。秦汉时期楚地巫术文化盛行，人们一直保持着用香薰来祭祀驱邪的习俗。据考证发现，楚地对香料的运用大体分为三个方面：一是祭祀驱邪；二是明志及增添生活情趣；三是医学用香。战国末期，楚国爱国诗人屈原写下千古名篇《离骚》，文中有大量关于江离、辟芷、秋兰、木兰、宿莽、申椒、菌桂、蕙、茝、荃等香草的描述。《离骚》是先秦时期论及香草、香木最多的典籍。"扈江离与辟芷兮，纫秋兰以为佩"，诗人将这些象征美好的香草披戴在身上，寄托自身高洁、高远的志向。仔细研读我们还会发现，《离骚》中提到的这三种香草都是常见的芳香类中药，江离即中药川芎；而辟芷即中药白芷；秋兰是常与"白芷"配对的惠兰，是中国的珍稀物种。兰草中有很多种类能够入药，马王堆出土医书《五十二病方》中即有以兰养生治病的记载，并详细介绍了其药用方法，书云："（齑）兰，以酒沃，饮其汁，以宰（滓）封其痏，数更之，以熏……"

马王堆一号墓出土的芳香类中药（辛夷、高良姜、藁本、桂皮、花椒、杜衡、茅香、佩兰、干姜）
Aromatic Chinese Medicines in Tomb 1: Xinyi (Flos Magnoliae), Gaoliangjiang (Rhizoma Alpiniae Officinarum), Gaoben (Rhizoma Ligustici), Guipi (Cinnamomum Tamala), Huajiao (Pericarpium Zanthoxyli), Duheng (Asarum Forbesii Maxim), Maoxiang (Hierochloe Odorata), Peilan (Herba Eupatorii), and Ganjiang (Zingiberis Rhizoma)

Sachets ward off evil and impurities, as well as avoid insect bites. The practice of wearing sachets among ancient Chinese people dates back to the pre-Qin period. The Chu region, situated in the Yangtze River Basin, is distinguished by its soaring mountains, ample rainfall, and lush vegetation. It is the main production area of spice plants, and the utilization of these plants here is particularly sophisticated. During the Qin and Han dynasties (221 B.C.—A.D. 220), witchcraft culture had been prevalent in the Chu region, and the custom of using aromatherapy to worship and ward off evil spirits had been maintained. According to research, the use of spices in the Chu region was roughly divided into three aspects: first, to offer sacrifices toward off evil spirits; second, to clarify aspirations and addingmore interest to life; third, to serve for medical purpose. In the late Warring States period, the patriotic poet Qu Yuan of the State of Chu wrote the timeless masterpiece *The Lament of Chu*, mentioning a lot of herbs such as Jiangli (Ligusticum Chuanxiong Hort), Bizhi (Angelica Dahurica), Qiulan(Cymbidium Ensifolium), Mulan(Magnolia Liliflora Desr), Sumang(Tripterygium Wilfordii), Shenjiao (Zanthoxyli Pericarpium), Jungui (Cortex Cinnamomi Macrophylli), Hui (Cymbidium Pumilum Rolfe), Chai (Dahurian Angelica), and Quan (Herba Girardiniae Palmtae). *The Lament of Chu*, a classic book that talks most about herbs and trees with fragrance in the pre Qin period, highlights the "perfumed grass and beauty", referring to things or people of loyalty to the sovereign and love for the country. "On my shoulders I wore Jiangli and Pizhi grass; by my side I tied the autumn orchids weaved as a garland."The poet draped these fragrant herbs symbolizing beauty on his body, embodying his noble and lofty aspirations. Upon careful study, we may find that the above-mentioned three herbs are common aromatic Chinese medicines: Jiangli is the Chinese medicine Chuanxiong (Ligusticum Chuanxiong Hort); Pizhiis the Chinese medicine Baizhi (Angelica Dahurica); autumn orchid is Huilan (Cymbidium faberi Rolfe),a rare species in China, often paired with Baizhi (Angelica Dahurica) in history. There are also many types of orchids that can be used as medicine. The medical book *Formulas for Fifty-two Diseases* unearthed in Mawangdui records the use of orchids for health preservation and treatment, providing a detailed introduction to their medicinal methods, as is stated in the book "Grind orchid into powder, soak it in alcohol, consume its juice, apply the residue on the sore, and change it multiple times."

佩兰是马王堆一号墓出土的具有代表性的中药，它不仅是出土香囊中的常用中药，更是出土药枕中的主要用料。药枕出土于北边箱，长 45 厘米，高 12 厘米，宽却只有 10 厘米。它的制作非常精美，上下两面用燕子图案的信期绣，两侧是香色地红茱萸锦纹，两端用的是高级绒毛棉。在修复中发现，枕头里填充的全是中药佩兰。佩兰是菊科植物佩兰的地上部分，又名鸡骨香、水香，它在古代又称"醒头草"，将其置于枕芯内可以起到芳香行散、开窍提神的作用。《神农本草经》记载佩兰"主利水道，杀蛊毒，辟不祥，久服益气，轻身不老，通神明"，指出佩兰具有利水、驱毒、辟秽、醒脑的功效，久服还能延年益寿。《本草经疏》记载佩兰"开胃除恶，清肺消痰，散郁结"。佩兰全草含挥发油 1.5% ~ 2%，气味特别芳香，加之性平味辛，具有很好的芳香化湿、醒脾和胃、清暑辟秽的作用。中国民间一直流传有"端午节，天气热；五毒醒，不安宁"的谚语，端午节佩戴香囊便成为一种防疫禳灾的民俗。佩兰的药用价值可以与水浴的保健功能相结合，加之其芳香的气味使人喜爱，在中国先秦至中唐这一历史阶段曾流行"浴兰汤"的习俗。屈原的《楚辞·九歌》里就有"浴兰汤兮沐芳"的叙述，西汉《大戴礼》记载"午日以兰汤沐浴"，记载了端午时节以佩兰煎水沐浴，防治皮肤病的习俗。现代研究发现，佩兰的挥发油可以抑菌杀菌，达到预防和治疗多种夏季皮肤病的目的，同时还有祛风止痛、舒筋活络等作用。

马王堆一号墓出土的黄褐绢地"长寿绣"枕头
Ochre-Colored Silk Pillow with "Changshou Embroidery" in Tomb 1

黄褐绢地"长寿绣"枕头填充的中药材佩兰
Peilan (Herba Eupatorii) from the Ochre-Colored Silk Pillow with "Changshou Embroidery"

Peilan (Herba Eupatorii) is a representative medicine unearthed in Tomb 1. It is not only a commonly used medicinal herb in the unearthed sachet, but also the main material used for the unearthed medicinal pillow. The medicinal pillow was unearthed in the northern chamber, measuring 45 centimeters in length, 12 centimeters in height, but only 10 centimeters in width. It's making is very exquisite, with a swallow pattern on both sides with "xinqi embroidery[5]" and the "red cornel-patterned brocade with incense color coating[6]" on both sides. The two ends are made of high-quality plush cotton. The pillow is filled entirely with Peilan (Herba Eupatorii), the aboveground part of the Peilan plant, also known as "chicken bone fragrance" or "water fragrance". It was named as the "mind clearing grass" in ancient times since putting it inside the pillow can unblock impediment, open orifices, and refresh mind with the aroma. The *Shennong's Herbal Classic* states, "It is utilized to facilitate the waterways, eradicate parasitic worms, and repel malevolent spirits.Prolonged usage can tonify qi, render the body agile and youthful, and enhance spiritual awareness." Here, Peilan (Herba Eupatorii) is believed to promote diuresis, expel toxins, dispel impurities, keep the mind clear, and potentially prolong life. The *Synopsis of Materia Medica* also states that, "Peilan (Herba Eupatorii)is known to stimulate appetite, eliminate pathogenic factors, clear the lungs, and dissolve phlegm, as well as disperse stagnation." The whole plant of Peilan contains approximately 1.5%—2% of volatile oil, which possessed a particularly fragrant aroma. Furthermore, it is characterized by the flat property and pungent flavour, exhibiting good aromatic properties and dampness-relieving effects. It is known as to regulate the spleen and stomach, clear heat, and eliminate impurities. In Chinese folklore, there is a saying that goes, "During the Dragon Boat Festival, the weather is hot, and the five venomous creatures[7] stir, causing unrest." As a result, wearing sachets during the festival has become a folk custom for preventing epidemics and disasters. The medicinal value of orchids, combined with the health benefits of water baths, coupled with the aroma, led to the popular custom of "bathing in orchid soup"during the historical period from pre Qin to mid Tang dynasties in China. The chapter of "Nine Songs" in *The Song of Chu* by Qu Yuan states, "Bathed in sweet flowers and orchid-scented dews" , while *the Rites by Da Dai* [8] in the Western Han Dynasty states, "On the Dragon Boat Festival, people take a herbal bath with orchid." Both of the two writings documents the custom of herbal bathing with Peilan (Herba Eupatorii) during the Dragon Boat Festival to prevent and treat skin diseases. Modern research has also discovered that the volatile oil of Peilan (Herba Eupatorii) possess the ability to inhibit and eliminate bacteria, thereby achieving the purpose of preventing and treating various skin diseases commonly encountered during summer. Additionally, it offers certain health benefits such as dispelling wind, alleviating pain, relaxing tendons, and harmonizing meridians.

---

[5] Xinqi embroidery is a type of embroidery from the Western Han Dynasty, renowned for its unique patterns and craftsmanship. This embroidery was mainly unearthed from the Mawangdui Han Dynasty Tombs, making it an important physical material for studying clothing and arts and crafts during the Western Han Dynasty. The name Xinqi embroidery has two origins: one is that three sachets, a pair of gloves, and a wrapper for a nine-compartment box embroidered with this pattern were all referred to as Xinqi embroidery in the inventory; the other is that the long-tailed birds in the embroidery resemble swallows, which are migratory birds that migrate south and north regularly, symbolizing that loyalty can express intentions, and faith can be expected in the long run, hence the name Xinqi embroidery.

[6] Red cornel-patterned brocade with incense color is the name of a type of brocade unearthed from the Mawangdui Han Dynasty Tombs. The pattern is composed of freehand flowers and diamond-shaped dots, arranged in a straight strip.

[7] The five venomous creatures includes venomous snakes, scorpions, toads, centipedes, and spiders (or lizards).

[8] Da is an honorific term used to show respect and reverence for Dai De, who had profound achievements in the field of ritual studies and exerted a far-reaching impact on the development of later generations' ritual studies.

马王堆一号汉墓中出土了一批中药材，佩兰只是其中的一种。至今尚可辨认的中药还有花椒、高良姜、茅香、藁本、桂皮、杜衡等 10 余种，分别存放于药袋、香囊、枕头和熏炉之中。从三号汉墓出土的彩绘陶熏炉高 13.3 厘米，口径 11.2 厘米，盖上有镂孔，以便发散熏烟，炉内装有高良姜、茅香、藁本和辛夷等中药。一号汉墓出土的竹熏罩，高 21 厘米，底径 30 厘米，口径 10 厘米，使用时罩在装有中药的熏炉上。炉内药物徐徐燃烧，缕缕青烟通过外面蒙着的细绢均匀地散发，阵阵清香扑鼻而至。花椒性热味辛，香气浓烈，含挥发油，有小毒，能温中散寒，止痛，燥湿，杀虫。高良姜性热味辛，能温中散寒，行气止痛，所含挥发油具有抗血栓和抑菌的功效。茅香性温味辛、甘，能疏风祛寒，温中止痛，止泻驱蛔，所含挥发油具有抑菌杀菌作用。这些出土中药大多归于辛香发散类药品，具有行气祛湿、通气健脾、防腐杀菌等功效。因此，它们在日常生活中可以发挥如下作用：一是改善室内空气，使空气变得清新怡人；二是杀菌消毒，消除秽浊；三是镇静安神，有利于睡眠。在西汉时代，熏香也是改善室内环境卫生的有效措施之一，尤其对湖南而言，湖南在古代被称为"卑湿之地"，《史记·货殖列传》中载有"江南卑湿，丈夫早夭"的说法。因此，对长期面临湿气和瘴气威胁的人们来说，用中药熏香能够起到预防疾病、除秽保健的作用。

马王堆三号墓出土的彩绘陶熏炉
Painted Pottery Smoking Furnace in Tomb 3

马王堆一号汉墓出土的竹熏罩
Bamboo Fumigation Cover in Tomb 1

A batch of Chinese medicinal herbs were unearthed from Tomb 1 besides Peilan (Herba Eupatorii). There were more than 10 recognizable medicines, including Huajiao (Pericarpium Zanthoxyli), Gaoliangjiang (Rhizoma Alpiniae Officinarum), Maoxiang (Hierochloe Odorata), Gaoben (Rhizoma Ligustici), Guipi (Cinnamomum Tamala), Duheng (Asarum Forbesii Maxim), and others, which were respectively stored in medicinal bags, sachets, pillows, or fumigators. The painted pottery smoking furnace unearthed in Tomb 3 was 13.3 centimeters high and 11.2 centimeters in diameter. It was covered with hollowed out holes to disperse the smoke. The furnace contained Gaoliangjiang (Rhizoma Alpiniae), Maoxiang (Hierochloe Odorata), Gaoben (Rhizoma Ligustici), and Xinyi (Flos Magnoliae), etc. The bamboo fumigation cover unearthed from Tomb1 was 21 centimeters high, with a bottom diameter of 30 centimeters and a diameter of 10 centimeters.It was used by placing it over a smoking pot containing Chinese herbs.The medicine inside the furnace slowly burned, and wisps of green smoke were evenly distributed through the thin silk covering the outside, emitting a refreshing fragrance. Huajiao (Pericarpium Zanthoxyli) possesses a hot property and pungent flavour, along with a potent aroma, containing volatile oil. It exhibits mild toxicity, yet can warm the body, dispel cold, relieve pain, dry dampness, and kill parasites. Gaoliangjiang (Rhizoma Alpiniae Officinarum), with its hot property and pungent flavour, warms the interior to dispel cold, promots qi circulation and alleviates pain. Additionally, the volatile oil it contained exhibits antithrombotic and antibacterial effects.Maoxiang (Hierochloe Odorata), characterized by its warm property and pungent flavour, effectively dispels wind and cold, warms the interior to relieve pain, checks diarrhea, and eliminats roundworms. The volatile oil it contains has antibacterial and bactericidal effects. The majority of these unearthed Chinese medicines are the pungent and fragrant medicines, known for their ability to promote qi circulation, eliminate dampness, enhance the spleen function, and provide anticorrosion and sterilization benefits. To sum up, they can play the following roles in daily life: first, they can refresh indoor air to make it pleasant; second, they can sterilize and disinfect, eliminating foul odors; third, they have a calming and soothing effect, which is conducive to rest and sleep. In the Western Han Dynasty, incense was also one of the effective measures to improve indoor environmental hygiene. It was especially effective for inhabitants in Hunan, known as the "low-lying and damp area" in ancient times. The Biography of Merchants and Trade in the *Records of the Grand Historian* says, "The southern region is low-lying and damp, and men there tend to die young." Therefore, by utilizing incense of Chinese medicines to purify and enhance overall health, individuals who were chronically exposed to dampness and miasma threats could be protected from various illnesses.

一缕药香绕千年，氤氲满室保安康。中国民间至今都流行着用艾叶、忍冬藤等简便易得的中药煮水沐浴，防治皮肤病的习俗。时至今日，薰香已成为一种风靡全球的美容、保健、解压方法，通过按摩、吸入、热敷、浸泡、蒸熏等方式，帮助人们在芳香治疗中重建身心平衡。现代香薰中的主要成分——精油，很多是从名贵中药材中提炼出来的，将精油涂抹身体各个部位，通过按摩等方式使之渗透到皮肤里层，随着血液循环将其中的有效成分运送至全身，帮助人们调节身心状态，防治相关疾病。薰香自古以来就是中国人的一种生活方式，而今它正以独特的疗效和雅致的文化融入现代人的健康生活之中。

A wisp of herbal scent, lingering since ancient times, fills the room with its essence, protecting health and minds. The Chinese folk tradition persists in advocating the boiling of water with accessible Chinese medicinal herbs, such as Aiye (Artemisiae Argyi Folium) and Jinyinhua (Lonicerae Japonicae Flos) vine, for preventing and treating skin diseases. Nowadays, aromatherapy has gained widespread popularity as a beauty, health care, and stress relief technique worldwide. Through practices like massage, inhalation, hot compress, soaking, and steaming, it aids individuals in restoring their physical and mental equilibrium. Essential oils, the main components used by modern aromatherapy, are frequently extracted from valuable Chinese medicinal herbs. These oils, when applied to various parts of the body, can penetrate into the inner layers of the skin through acupoints. Circulating through the vessels, they effectively regulate people's physical and mental states, preventing and treating related diseases. Deeply rooted in Chinese culture since antiquity, aromatherapy is now effortlessly merging into the modern lifestyle, imparting its distinctive therapeutic advantages and exhibiting exquisite cultural nuances.

# 出土竹笥中的饮食奥义

**Dietary Secrets Within the Items in Unearthed Bamboo Baskets**

# 道县

中国是世界农业的主要起源地之一，而湖湘这片钟灵毓秀之地与水稻结下了奇妙的缘分。湖湘大地上发现过各个时期的稻作文化遗址，如道县玉蟾岩、怀化高庙、澧县城头山等。湖南省道县玉蟾岩遗址发掘出了距今约14000年的人工栽培稻标本，刷新了人类最早栽培水稻的历史纪录。同时，这里还出土了距今约12000年的原始陶片，因而被誉为"天下谷源，人间陶本"。因此，湖南是中国农耕文明的重要发源地之一，自古就流传着"湖广熟，天下足"的谚语。湖南、湖北两省是中国主要的商品粮基地之一，战国时期长沙就是重要的粮食生产基地。率先掌握水稻种植和陶器使用的湖湘先民，用勤劳和智慧在这片丰饶富足的土地上，为湖南人种下了追求美好、热爱美食的文化基因。

China is recognized as one of the primary birthplaces of global agriculture. Hunan Province, renowned for its abundant natural beauty and fertile lands, has established a profound connection with rice. Numerous sites of rice farming in different historical periods have been discovered on the land of Hunan, such as Yuchanyan in Daoxian, Gaomiao in Huaihua, and Chengtou Mountain in Lixian. Artificially cultivated rice specimens, dating back approximately 14,000 years, have been excavated at Yuchanyan in Daoxian, breaking a new record for the earliest human cultivation of rice. Additionally, primitive pottery fragments about 12,000 years ago have been unearthed here, earning it the reputation of "the source of grains in the world and the origin of human pottery". Therefore, Hunan is recognized as one of the important birthplaces of Chinese agricultural civilization, and has long been known for the proverb, "A good harvest in Hunan and Hubei ensures abundant food throughout the country." Hunan and Hubei provinces together constitute one of the main commodity grain bases in China. During the Warring States period (475—221B.C.), Changsha was already an important grain production base. The early ancestors of Hunan were pioneers who first mastered rice cultivation and pottery usage, instilling cultural genes that embody a deep appreciation for beauty and gastronomy into this fertile land with their diligence and wisdom.

马王堆一号汉墓出土随葬品中不但有大量残留食品，还有食简、筷子、食器等，足以成为湖湘饮食文化的一张特色名片。这些随葬食物品类极多，大部分都盛放在竹笥和麻袋里，还有一部分盛放在陶器和漆器中。根据出土遣策记载，一号墓的菜单有近百道菜名。竹笥是由竹篾编织而成的盛物箱子。马王堆一号汉墓曾出土48个竹笥，里边装满了五花八门的随葬物品。根据竹笥外边拴着的竹简标注统计，这些竹笥中装有食品类30笥，中草药及其他植物茎类8笥，衣物及丝织品6笥，模型明器类4笥。初步推算，所有随葬品中食品类占到了60%左右，真正体现和突出了"民以食为天"这一特点。三号墓中的52个竹笥虽然已严重腐朽，但从保存的竹笥木牌来看，盛放食物的有40多笥，而三号墓遣策记载的菜名比一号墓还要丰富。

The funeral objects unearthed from Mawangdui Han Dynasty Tomb 1 comprise not only a large amount of leftover food, but also bamboo slips, chopsticks, and various food utensils. This collection serves as an emblematic representation of Hunan cuisine culture. There are a wide variety of burial food items, most of which are placed in bamboo basket or burlap bag, while others in pottery or lacquerware. According to the list of funeral objects, the menu found from Tomb 1 encompasses nearly a hundred dish names. From Tomb 1, a total of 48 skillfully crafted bamboo baskets, woven with bamboo strips and used for storage, were unearthed. Each basket was filled with a variety of funeral objects. According to the labeling statistics on bamboo slips tied outside the bamboo baskets, there are 30 baskets for food, eight for herbs and plant stems, six for clothing and silk products, and four for model artifacts for the dead. Among them, food accounts for about 60% of all funeral items, reflecting and highlighting the view of "Bread is the staff of life". In Tomb 3, the 52 bamboo baskets have been severely damaged or decayed. According to the preserved wooden tags of the baskets, over 40 of them are used for storing food. The dish names recorded in the list of funeral objects in Tomb 3 are even more abundant than those in Tomb 1.

马王堆汉墓出土的食品遣策（局部图）
Food List in Mawangdui Han Dynasty Tombs（Partial Picture）

马王堆一号墓出土的竹笥
Bamboo Basket in Tomb 1

马王堆一号墓出土的云纹漆鼎
Cloud-Patterned Lacquer Tripod in Tomb 1

云纹漆鼎出土时盛放有汤和莲藕片
Cloud-Patterned Lacquer Tripod Containing Slices of Lotus Root Soap when Unearthened

马王堆一号墓出土的彩绘陶鼎，内盛鸡骨
Painted Pottery Tripod Containing Chicken Bones in Tomb 1

　　从食品竹笥所装的食物判断，西汉时期的主、副食品非常丰富。主食有稻、麦、黍、粟、大豆、赤豆、麻子等谷物；副食有梨、梅、杨梅等果品，东葵、芥菜、竹笋、姜、藕等蔬菜，牛、羊、猪、狗、兔等兽类，以及各种鱼类、禽类，可谓五谷杂粮、飞禽走兽一应俱全。西汉时期不仅主、副食品种类繁多，烹调方法也很讲究。其中，主食有米饭、蒸饼、熬粥及米羹之类。烹调时使用的调料有盐、酱、糖、醋、蜜等，香料有茱萸、蕙、姜、榆叶、襄荷等。肉食品的烹调加工方法尤为精细而多样，包括羹、炙、煎、熬、蒸、濯、脍、脯、腊、菹等十余种。所谓羹即熬煮成浓汤或薄糊状的食物，种类多样，多为肉羹。例如，大羹是单纯用肉做成的，白羹是由米屑和肉做成的，巾羹是肉加堇菜或芹菜做成的，苦羹则指加了苦菜的肉羹。根据竹笥中的 312 枚竹简统计，记载各种肉羹的竹简有 29 枚之多，如"牛白羹""鹿肉芋白羹""鹿肉鲍鱼笋羹""鸡白羹瓠菜""狗巾羹（即狗肉芹菜羹）""狗苦羹（即狗肉苦菜羹）"等。狗肉是汉代人喜爱的食物，除"狗巾羹""狗苦羹"外，遣策上记载的还有犬肝炙（即烤狗肝）、犬其胁（即烤狗胁肉）等。中医学认为狗肉味甘咸，性温热，具有安五脏、暖腰膝、益肾壮阳、补益胃气的作用。现代研究还发现，狗肉能够有效改善血液循环，促进人体消化吸收。这些出土食品竹笥反映了中国古代人民高超的饮食智慧，为我们今天的摄食养生提供了有益的借鉴。

马王堆一号墓出土的"君幸食"狸纹漆盘
Leopard– Patterned Lacquer Tray Inscribed with "君幸食 (Enjoy Your Meal)" in Tomb 1

马王堆一号墓出土的"君幸酒"云纹漆耳杯
Cloud–Patterned Ear Cup Insribed with "君幸酒 (Enjoy Your Wine)" in Tomb 1

From the food items in bamboo baskets, it can be judged that the staple and non-staple foods in the Western Han Dynasty were exceptionally abundant. The staple foods included rice, wheat, millet, chestnuts, soybeans, adzuki beans, and sesame seeds; and the non-staple foods included fruits and vegetables likes pears, plums, and prunes, malva crispa, mustard greens, bamboo shoots, ginger, and lotus roots. There were also cattle, sheep, pigs, dogs, rabbits, as well as fish, poultry, and other meat food. To sum up, in the Western Han Dynasty, the refined and coarse grains and cereals, birds and beasts were all available.Besides, cooking methods in this period were sophisticated. Among them, the staple foods could be cooked as rice, steamed cake, porridge, rice soup, and so on. The seasonings used in cooking included salt, soy sauce, sugar, vinegar, honey, and others, and the spices included cornus officinalis, basil leaves, ginger, elm leaves, zingiber mioga, etc. Particularly, the cooking of meat products was sophisticated and varied, including stewing, baking, frying, boiling, steaming, instant-boiling, bruising, drying up, curing, mince, and so on. The so-called "geng" refers to food that is boiled into a thick soup or thin paste, with various types, in which meat geng is the most common. Among them, "da geng" was made purely from meat, "bai geng" from rice crumbs and meat, "jin geng" from meat with spinach or celery, and "ku geng" from meat with bitter vegetables. According to 312 bamboo slips attached to the baskets, there were as many as 29 bamboo slips recording various types of meat geng, such as "beef white geng", "venison and taro white geng", "venison abalone and bamboo geng", "chicken white geng", "dog vegetable geng", "dog bitter vegetable geng", and so on. Dog meat was the favorite food of the people in the Han Dynasty. In addition to the above records, the list of funeral objects also included dishes such as roasted dog liver and roasted dog ribs. According to CM, dog meat had the sweet and salty flavour, warm and hot property, so eating it can comfort the five zang organs, warm the waist and knees, tonify the kidneys and strengthen yang, and nourish the stomach qi. Modern research has also found that dog meat can effectively improve blood circulation, digestion, and absorption. These unearthed bamboo baskets for food reflects the ancient Chinese people's wisdom on dietary, which provide a useful reference for today's dietary health preservation.

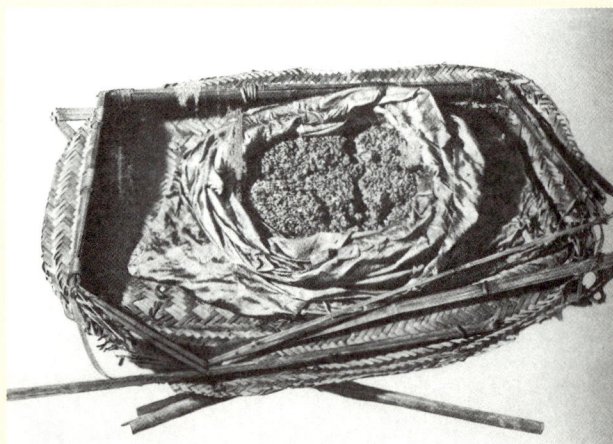

盛有豆类的竹笥
Bamboo Box Containing Beans

盛有蛋壳的竹笥
Bamboo Box Containing Eggshells

摄食养生是中医养生理论与实践的重要组成部分，《黄帝内经》时期就总结出了"五谷为养，五果为助，五畜为益，五菜为充，气味合而服之，以补精益气"的膳食配制原则。这种饮食搭配的养生智慧，从马王堆出土竹笥所盛的食品中可以窥见一斑。在我们的日常饮食中，"五谷""五果""五畜""五菜"应合理搭配，才能充分补充机体的气血精微物质，保障我们的健康。"精、气、神"乃人生三宝，其中"精"是人体生命的本源，而饮食所化生的水谷精微是人体精微物质的重要来源。因此，保持合理膳食，可以起到聚精养气的作用，有益于延年益寿。中医学的膳食主张乃"五谷为养长寿命，五果为助健脾胃，五畜为益丰肌肉，五菜为充足营养"。五谷即粳米、小豆（即绿豆）、小麦、大豆、黄黍（即玉米），这是中国人的传统主食。中医学认为"五谷最养脾，天生万物，独厚五谷"，原因是人体所需要的营养元素几乎都在五谷杂粮之中。五谷不仅可以作为食物，还可以入药用于疾病防治。譬如，粳米入药可补中益气、健脾和胃、除烦止渴、止泻；赤小豆入药则可清热解毒、消暑除烦、利水消肿；小麦更有"五谷之贵"的美誉，其养心安神、滋阴生津的功效对女性更年期调养大有裨益。五果即桃、李、

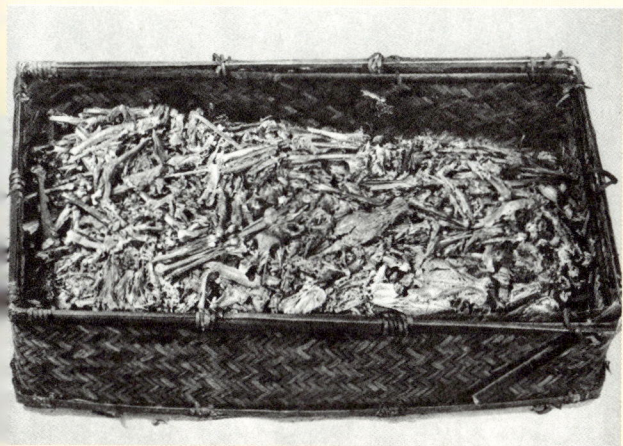

盛有雉骨的竹笥
Bamboo Box Containing Chicken Bones

杏、栗、枣，其蕴含的维生素、纤维素、有机酸、矿物质等对人体健康甚为重要，对某些疾病亦有一定的治疗作用。比如，素有"仙品""寿果"之称的桃，味甘微酸，性温，具有敛肺止汗、活血消积等功效，常被人们用作虚劳咳嗽及高血压动脉硬化患者的佐食。五畜即牛、羊、豕（猪）、鸡、犬，其肉是人体优质蛋白质的重要来源，含有人体必需的氨基酸，并能提供铁、铜、锌等微量元素。比如，猪肘、牛肘、羊肘、狗肘等各种肘，是马王堆汉墓出土竹笥所盛的肉类食物的重头戏。五菜即葵、藿、葱、薤、韭，蔬菜素有"维生素仓库"之称，能够满足人体的各种维生素需求，可以防治各种维生素缺乏导致的疾病，并具有防癌抗癌作用。中国民谚有"白菜豆腐保平安"的说法，看似平凡廉价的大白菜，因富含维生素C、钙质及纤维素，可以增进食欲、通肠排便、活血化瘀，起到预防痔疮的作用，并对胃及十二指肠溃疡有一定的辅助疗效。同时，白菜的根、茎、叶、籽都可入药疗疾。

Dietary health preservation is an important part of CM theory and practice regarding health preservation. Since the *Huangdi's Classic of Medicine* period, the dietary principle has been summarized as "Grains are the foundation of nutrition, providing the body with essential nutrients; fruits serve as a supplement, helping to replenish various nutrients needed by the body; meat can enhance the nourishing effect on the body; vegetables can be used as a complement to ensure a balanced nutrition. Combining the nutritional properties and benefits of these different types of food can nourish the body's essence and qi." The wisdom of dietary health preservation can also be glimpsed from the food stored in the bamboo baskets unearthed in Mawangdui. Accordingly, in daily lives, people should reasonably combine grains, fruits, meat, and vegetables to fully supplement the body's qi, blood, and essence, thereby ensuring health and longevity. "Essence, qi, and spirit " are known as the three treasures of life, among which "essence" is the origin of human life, and the subtle essence derived from food and water is an important source of human body essence. Therefore, maintaining a balanced diet can help preserve essence and cultivate qi, ultimately prolonging life. The dietary health preservation principles of CM are "grains are for nourishing longevity, fruits are for aiding digestion, meat for enhancing muscle growth, and vegetables for providing sufficient nutrition." Grains refer to rice, mung beans (green beans), wheat, soybeans, and millet (corn), which are the traditional staple foods of the Chinese people. CM believes that "grains nourish the spleen best, as they are the source of all things and rich in essential nutrients needed by the human body." The grains are not only used as food, but also can be used as the medicine for disease prevention and

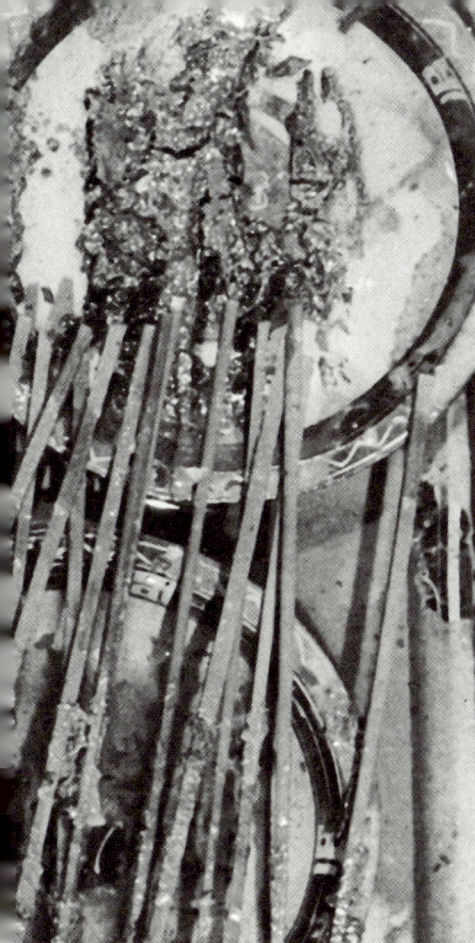

马王堆一号墓出土的摆放食物的云纹漆案
Cloud–Patterned Lacquer Tray for Placing Food in Tomb 1

treatment. For example, using polished rice can tonify qi of the spleen and stomach, strengthen the spleen and harmonize the stomach, relieve restlessness and thirst, and check diarrhea. And adzuki beans can clear heat and remove toxicity, relieve summer heat and restlessness, induce diuresis to alleviate edema. Wheat is highly regarded as one of the most valuable grains, with effects of nourishing the heart, calming the mind, nourishing yin, and generating body fluid, which are of great benefit to female menopause recuperation. Fruits, including peaches, plums, apricots, chestnuts, and dates, are rich in essential nutrients such as vitamins, fiber, organic acids, and minerals, which play a crucial role in promoting human health and possess certain therapeutic effects on specific diseases. For example, peaches, known as "immortal product"and "longevity fruit", have a sweet and slightly sour flavour, a warm nature, and possess effects such as astringing the lungs, stopping sweating, circulating blood, and resolving masses. They are often used as a supplementary food for patients with deficiency, fatigue, cough, hypertension, and arteriosclerosis. Meat products, including beef, mutton, pork, chicken, and dog meat, are significant sources of high-quality protein for the human body. They contain essential amino acids that are necessary for the body and provide trace elements such as iron, copper, and zinc. For example,various types of knuckles such as pork knuckle, beef knuckle, mutton knuckle, and dog knuckle, are the highlights of the meat products stored in bamboo baskets unearthed from the Mawangdui Han Dynasty Tombs. The vegetables, such as Chinese kale, mung bean sprouts, scallion, garlic chives, and leek, are known as the "vitamin warehouse" and can meet the body's needs for various vitamins. They prevent and treat diseases caused by vitamin deficiencies, and also prevent and resist cancer. There is a Chinese proverb that goes, "Chinese cabbage and tofu ensure safety." Although cabbage is ordinary and cheap, it is rich in vitamin C, calcium, and fiber, and can enhance appetite, promote bowel movements, eliminate congestion, and prevent hemorrhoids. It also has a certain auxiliary therapeutic effect on gastric and duodenal ulcers.Furthermore, the roots, stems, leaves, and seeds of Chinese cabbage can all be used for medicinal treatment.

药食同源，凡膳皆药，中医学认为许多食物同时也是药物。比如，我们常见的山药、山楂、乌梅、木瓜、百合、龙眼肉、蜂蜜等，它们既是可口的食物，又具有防病治病的妙用。出土竹笥里的饮食奥义，也是现代健康生活的智慧之源。坚持"五谷""五果""五畜""五菜"多元搭配，均衡饮食，以古老的智慧帮助我们养成健康的饮食习惯，有益于我们保持身心平衡，增强身体功能。

Medicine and food share the same origin, and all foods can be medicinal. CM advocates that many foods can serve as medicines. For example, the common food, like yam, hawthorn, dark plum, papaya, lilium brownii, longan meat, honey, and others, are not only the delicious food,but also possess the function of preventing and treating diseases. The dietary secrets discovered within the items from unearthed bamboo baskets are also the source of wisdom for modern healthy life. Adhering to a diverse and balanced diet that includes grains, fruits, meat products, and vegetables, people can maintain physical and mental balance and enhance bodily functions through healthy eating habits, guided by ancient wisdom.

起居调摄守护

# 健康人生

The Adjustment of Daily Routine
for Maintenance of a Healthy Life

马王堆一号汉墓出土了基本完整的丝、麻织物和服饰百余件，分装在 6 个竹笥中。而三号墓中的高级丝织物有 11 箱，其数量和品种比一号墓还多。这些丝织品包括印花、绣花和织锦的丝绸被子及绣花枕头、枕巾等，衣物则包括长袍、禅衣、裙子、裤子、袍缘、鞋子、手套等多个品类。其中最令人叹为观止的是一号墓出土的素纱禅衣，衣长 128 厘米，通袖长 190 厘米，称得上是宽袍大袖。这件"薄若蝉翼""轻若烟雾"的衣裳，仅重 49 克，折叠后甚至可以放入火柴盒中，反映了西汉高超的纱织水平。马王堆汉墓随葬衣物款式丰富、衣料多样、色彩瑰丽，反映出当时的贵族阶层对衣着服饰方面的考究和追求，也是西汉初期人们生活起居方面的一处折射。中国人素来重视起居养生，将养生调摄理念贯穿衣食住行之中，穿衣戴帽这些看似寻常的事件却暗藏着深厚的养生学问。

马王堆三号墓
出土的衣物遣
策（局部图）
Clothes List in
Tomb 3 (Partial
Picture)

马王堆一号墓出土的朱红丝绵袍
Vermilion Silk and Cotton–Patterned Robe in Tomb 1

马王堆一号墓出土的印花敷彩绛红纱锦袍
Printed and Colored Crimson Brocade Robe in Tomb 1

马王堆一号墓出土的素纱禅衣
Plain Unlined Gauze Gown in Tomb 1

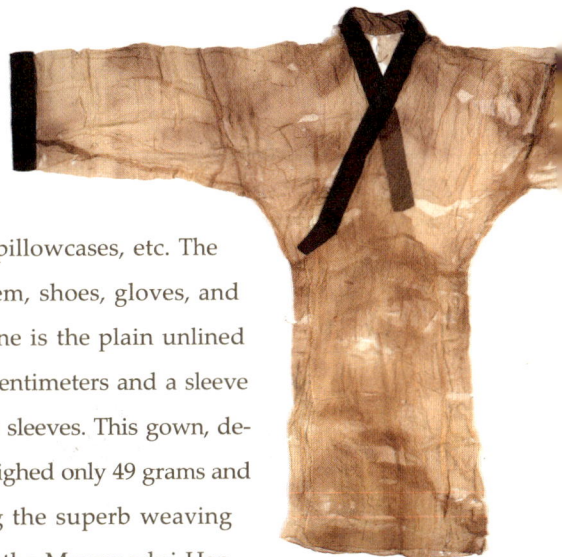

More than one hundred pieces of basically intact silk, linen fabrics, and clothing were unearthed from Mawangdui Han Dynasty Tomb 1, packed separately in six bamboo baskets. In Tomb 3, there are 11 boxes of high-quality silk fabrics, with greater quantity and variety than those in Tomb 1. These silk fabrics include printed, embroidered, and brocaded silk quilts, as well as embroidered pillows, pillowcases, etc. The clothing include robes, unlined garments, skirts, pants, hem, shoes, gloves, and many other categories. Among them, the most stunning one is the plain unlined gauze gown unearthed from Tomb 1.With a length of 128 centimeters and a sleeve length of 190 centimeters, it is indeed a wide robe with large sleeves. This gown, described as "thin as a cicada wing" and as "light as smoke", weighed only 49 grams and can even be folded and placed in a matchbox, representing the superb weaving skills in the Western Han Dynasty. The funeral clothes in the Mawangdui Han Dynasty Tombs are rich in styles, diverse in materials, and magnificent in colors, reflecting the exquisite taste and pursuit of the aristocracy in clothing and accessories at that time, which is also a reflection of daily life in the early Western Han Dynasty. Chinese people have always attached great importance to health preservation in their daily life, integrating health preservation and adjustment into clothing, food, housing, and transportation. Actually, the seemingly ordinary acts of dressing and hat-wearing conceal profound knowledge of health preservation.

《脉法》是马王堆汉墓出土的现今发现最早的脉学理论古籍，内容主要涉及灸法和砭法两个方面。其中，《脉法》在灸法中指出"圣人寒头而煖（暖）足"，因而提出"治病者取有余而益不足也"，这是最早提出中医学"虚实补泻"理念的古代医籍之一。这一原则用于指导养生就简称为"寒头暖足"。所谓寒头，就是要主动适应自然温度的变化，尽量保持头部的寒凉。而"暖足"，则是要顺应四时变化，及时"祛寒就温"，让足部保持温暖。根据考证，许多古医书中提到了"寒头"与"暖足"，但《脉法》是首次将"寒头暖足"四个字紧密联系在一起立论的。中医学认为，头为诸阳之会，即体内所有阳经循行汇聚的地方。从人体十二经脉和三百六十五络脉的循行走向来看，阴精、气血（特别是阳气）均上走于头面，人的五官也都集中在头面部位。因此，头部所凝聚的阳气最为充盛，由此有了"寒头"的养生之理。我们常有这样的体验，当头面部发热时常会感到昏沉、心烦。因此，"寒头"养生要注意掌握"三法"：一是要常洗冷水脸。长时间用脑过度，会出现脑门发热、头昏脑涨的不适感，此时用冷水洗脸，可以达到放松精神、提高思维能力的效果。长期坚持用冷水洗脸，可以预防感冒，尤其在冬天可以提高人体抵御风寒的能力。二是不要蒙头睡觉，否则醒后易因缺氧而出现头晕、胸闷、乏力、精神不振等，还可诱发噩梦。现代研究表明，让头部保持相对低温有利于改善睡眠。三是戴帽要适时，应让头部尽量适应自然温度变化，不必在略有降温和有凉意时急于戴帽，要坚持适度原则。

马王堆一号墓出土的绢地"信期绣"手套
Silk Gloves with "Xinqi Embroidery" in Tomb 1

马王堆一号墓出土的朱红色菱纹罗手套
Silk Gloves with Vermilion Rhombus Pattern in
Tomb 1

The *Treatment Methods based on Meridians*, unearthed from the Mawangdui Han Dynasty Tombs, the earliest ancient book on meridian theory discovered so far, mainly covers two parts: moxibustion and stone needling therapy. It points out in the moxibustion therapy part that "the sages always keep the heads cold and the feet warm", and thus proposes "the medical practitioners always reduce the excess and supplement the deficiency when treating diseases". It is the earliest ancient medical book that has established the concept of "reducing the excess while supplementing the deficiency" in CM. And this principle has been referred to as "keeping the head cold and the feet warm" when used to guide health preservation. The so-called "keeping the head cold" is to actively adapt to changes in natural temperature and try to keep the head cold, while "keeping the feet warm" means following the changes of the four seasons and keeping the feet warm by timely "dispelling cold and warming". According to research, the concepts of "keeping the head cold"and "keeping the feet warm" have been mentioned separately in many ancient medical books, but it is the *Treatment Methods based on Meridians* that first closely links the two concepts to establish a theory. CM believes that the head is the the place where all kinds of yang meet, that is, the place where all yang meridians in the body converge. From the perspective of the circulation direction of the 12 meridians and 365 collaterals of the human body, it can be observed that yin essence, qi and blood, especially yang qi, all ascend to the head and face where our five sense organs are also distributed on. Accordingly, the head is where the most abundant yang qi gathers, thus creating the health preservation theory of "keeping the head cold". We often have such an experience that when our head and face are hot, we may feel drowsy and irritable. Therefore, how do we "keep the head cold"? It is crucial to grasp the following "three methods". One is to wash face with cold water regularly. After a long period of excessive mental exertion, one may experience forehead fever and dizziness. At this time, washing face with cold water can relax and improve thinking ability. Additionally, long-term adherence to washing face with cold water can prevent colds as well as improve the body's ability to resist wind and cold, especially in winter. The second is to avoid sleeping with your head covered, otherwise, dizziness, chest tightness, fatigue, listlessness, and other symptoms may easily occur due to hypoxia after waking up, and it may also induce nightmares. Modern research also suggests that keeping the head at a relatively low temperature is beneficial for sleep. The third method is to wear a hat at the right time, allowing the head to adapt to natural temperature changes as much as possible. There is no need to rush to wear a hat when there is a slight drop in temperature or cooling sensation to adhere to the principle of moderation.

关于"暖足"，中国民间一直流传着"寒从足下起"的说法，这是因为"阴脉者，集于足下，而聚于足心"。人体阴经的经气集中在足底，聚会于足心，所以阴气并走于下部容易导致足底寒冷。同时，足少阴肾经、足太阴脾经两条与生命"先天之本""后天之本"紧密联系的重要经脉都起始于足部，这表明足部保养对生命健康是非常重要的。暖足养生要做好"三件事"：第一件事是泡足，每天泡足 20 分钟，可以达到治疗疾病、强身健体的效果。热水泡足具有促进气血运行、温煦脏腑、通经活络的作用，可以调节内脏器官功能，促进周身血液循环，使毛细血管通畅，改善全身组织营养状况，加强机体新陈代谢作用，舒缓精神紧张。第二件事是按足，通过推拿按摩足部的病理反射区或经穴、奇穴等部位，可以调整阴阳、调和气血、调节脏腑，达到防病治病的目的。按足重点关注两个穴位——足三里和涌泉。足三里具有调理脾胃、扶正培元、通经活络等功效，而涌泉对晕厥、头顶痛、眩晕、中暑、神经衰弱、高血压等具有治疗作用。通过长期反复按揉，或者针刺、艾灸等方式刺激上述两个穴位，对温通血脉、强健身体大有裨益。第三件事是健足，正如中国古语所言："饭后百步走，活到九十九。"走路的方式有很多，比较特殊的包括前脚掌走、矮身走、脚跟走、向后走、太极步、走石子等，都具有独特的防病治病效果。

马王堆一号墓出土的青丝履
Cyan Silk Shoes in Tomb 1

马王堆一号墓出土的绛紫绢袜
Dark Purple Silk Socks in Tomb 1

for "keeping the feet warm", there is a Chinese saying that goes, "Cold starts from the feet." This is because that "yin meridians gather at the feet and converge at the soles", causing yin qi to flow towards the lower parts of the body, which subsequently leads to coldness in the feet. Meanwhile, two crucial meridians are closely linked to the "congenital foundation" and "postnatal foundation" of life, i.e., the kidney meridian of foot-Shaoyin and the spleen meridian of foot-Taiyin, both starting from the feet, further underscoring the significance of foot care for maintaining good health. Just like the three methods for "keeping the head cold", there are also three essential ways for "keeping the feet warm". The first one is "foot soaking". Soaking feet for 20 minutes daily can contribute to disease treatment and physical strengthening. Warm water soaking can promote qi and blood circulation, warm zang-fu organs, unblock meridians and collaterals, thereby regulating the functions of zang-fu organs, promoting systemic blood circulation, increasing capillary patency, improving the nutritional status of body tissues, strengthening the body's metabolism, and relieving mental stress. The second way is"foot reflexology", which involves massaging the pathological reflex zones, meridian points, and extra points on the feet to balance yin and yang, harmonize qi and blood, and regulate the functions of zang-fu organs for purpose of preventing or treating disease. When massaging the feet, two acupoints deserve special attention, namely, Zusanli (ST36) and Yongquan (KI1).Acupoint massage at Zusanli (ST36) can regulate and harmonize the spleen and stomach, reinforce the healthy qi to strengthen the body, unblock meridians and collaterals, while massage at Yongquan (KI1) has therapeutic effects on conditions such as syncope, headache, dizziness, heatstroke, neurasthenia, and hypertension. Long-term repeated massage, acupuncture, or moxibustion at the two acupoints is beneficial for warming and unblocking blood vessels and strengthening the body. The third way is "foot excercising".As the ancient Chinese saying goes, "A walk after dinner will help you live to ninety-nine." There are various ways of "foot excercising", each with its unique effects in preventing and treating diseases,including walking on the front soles, walking in a low posture, walking on the heels, walking backwards, walking in Tai Chi steps[9], and walking on cobblestones.

---

[9] Tai Chi step is the basic footwork of Tai Chi boxing, characterized by its soft overcoming hardness and slow, smooth movements, which helps regulate breathing and enhance body balance and inner strength.

除"寒头暖足"的智慧外，马王堆医学在生活起居方面的健康理念还体现在多个方面，比如出土的药枕是古人注重睡眠养生的一个实证。西汉文学家司马相如在《长门赋》中云："抟芬若以为枕兮，席荃兰而茝香。"诗中的"若"，即"杜若"，别称"竹叶莲"，是一种香气浓郁的药草，故又称"芬若"。以芬若制作枕头，既可闻香又可清热解毒，由此可断定，"以药为枕"在西汉时候就已流行。马王堆一号汉墓出土的药枕是我国目前见到的最早的药枕，以佩兰填塞制作药枕的枕芯，既有芳香化湿、抑菌辟秽的作用，又具养血安眠的功效。中医学认为，头为诸阳之会、精明之府，气血皆上聚于头部，头与全身经络腧穴有密切联系。使用药枕可以使药物直接作用于头部，从而发挥其治病祛邪、平衡气血、调节阴阳的功效。药枕还可通过药物的芳香挥发渗入血脉之中，沿血脉达病所，发挥调节气机、协调脏腑的治病效果；或发挥"通关窍、利滞气"的作用，促进神经、肌肉与关节功能协调。中国古代最为流行的药枕当属菊枕，即以菊花、菊叶作为枕芯的填充料。古人喜欢用菊枕，主要取其清热疏风、益肝明目等特性。例如，清代慈禧太后每到秋菊怒放时，总要命人摘取大朵菊花，撕出花瓣晒干揉碎，填进布袋充作枕芯。菊花中所含的微量龙脑、樟脑、菊油环酮可挥发出"药气"，刺激头颈皮肤，能起到活血化瘀、通利筋骨的作用。菊枕还可防治头晕眼花，夜晚催人酣睡，翌晨起床使人神清目明。故中国民谚有云："菊枕常年置头下，老来身轻眼不花。"

马王堆一号墓出土的绢地"乘云绣"枕巾
Silk Pillow Cover with "Chengyun Embroidery" in Tomb 1

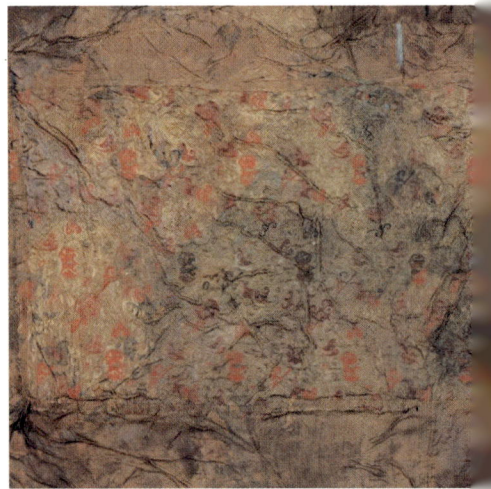

马王堆一号墓出土的黄褐色对鸟菱纹绮地"乘云绣"枕巾
Ochre-Colored and Rhombus-Patterned Brocade Pillow Cover Featuring "Chengyun Embroidery" and Paired Bird Design in Tomb 1

Besides the wisdom of "keeping the head cold and feet warm", the health concept of Mawangdui medicine in daily life is also reflected in multiple aspects. The unearthed medicinal pillow is an empirical example of emphasizing sleep health. Sima Xiangru, a litterateur in the Western Han Dynasty, wrote in his poem *Changmen Fu*, "Pillowed with pressed Fenruo, and seated on a mat spread with Tulan, how fragrant it is!" The "Fenruo" in the poem refers to "Duruo", also known as "Zhuyelian (Polliajaponica Thunb)", a kind of fragrant herb, hence the name "Fenruo". Using Fenruo to make pillows can not only give off a sweet fragrance but also clear heat and remove toxins, indicating that "using medicine as a pillow" was already popular in the Western Han Dynasty. The medicinal pillow unearthed in Mawangdui Han Dynasty Tomb 1 has been the earliest one discovered in China. The core of pillow is filled with Peilan (Eupatorii Herba), which has the functions of transforming dampness, antibacterial, and deodorizing, as well as nourishing blood and improving sleep. CM believes that the head is the center of all yang meridians and the residence of intelligence, and the qi and blood all gather on the head, which is closely connected with the meridians and acupoints of the whole body. The medicinal pillows allows the medicine to directly act on the head, thereby curing diseases and eliminating pathogenic factors, balancing qi and blood, as well as regulating yin and yang. Additionally, the medicinal pillow can allow the aroma of the herbs to penetrate into the bloodstream, making it reach the affected area along the blood vessels, regulate qi movement, coordinate the zang and fu organs to treat diseases. It can as well exert the effect of "opening orifices and smoothing qi stagnation", promoting the coordination function of nerve, muscle and joint. Undoubtedly, the most popular medicinal pillow in ancient China was chrysanthemum pillow, with chrysanthemums and chrysanthemum leaves as filling materials for the pillow core. The Chinese ancients favored chrysanthemum pillows mainly due to their characteristics of clearing heat, removing wind and benefiting the liver and brightening the eyes. For example, every autumn when the chrysanthemums bloomed, the Empress Dowager Cixi[10] of the Qing Dynasty would order people to pick chrysanthemums in full blossom, tear out their petals, dry and crush them, then fill them into a cloth bag to make a pillow core. The micro-amounts of borneol, camphor, and chrysanthemum oil ketone contained in the chrysanthemums emit a "medicinal aroma" to stimulate the skin of the head and neck, which can promote blood circulation to remove blood stasis and invigorate sinews and bones. Chrysanthemum pillows can also prevent and treat dizziness and blurred vision, promoting sound sleep at night and making people feel refreshed when they wake up the next morning. Hence goes a Chinese proverb, "With a chrysanthemum pillow under the head all year round, one will stay fit and have good eyesight even in old age."

---

[10] The Empress Dowager Cixi was an important political figure in the late Qing Dynasty, who controlled the imperial government for 48 years and had a profound impact on the politics of the late Qing Dynasty.

辛追药枕今犹在，起居养生保安康。由湖南博物院和湖南省中医药大学组建的研究团队针对出土药枕的原物制作材料和用途，依据出土医书《养生方》《脉法》的记载及相关养生理论，潜心研究，精工打造，创造性地研发出"马王堆"千金养生枕产品。"马王堆"千金养生枕自 2008 年试销以来，以其独特的养生文化内涵和卓越的健康养护品质，受到社会各界的好评，到 2009 年底就获得了国家文物局和市级多个奖项，现已成为湖南对外交流的一张名片。

The medicinal pillow once used by Xin Zhui is still in existence today.It keeps people maintaining a healthy lifestyle as it ever did. Nowadays, the research team,organized by Hunan Provincial Museum and Hunan University of Chinese Medicine,have been conducting intensive research, focusing on the original materials and uses of unearthed medicinal pillows and based on the records and health theories in the unearthed medical books the *Health Preservation Recipes* and the *Treatment Methods based on Meridians*. The team has creatively developed and crafted a series of "Mawangdui" health pillow products. The "Mawangdui"Qianjin[11] health pillow, since its trial sale in 2008, has been highly praised by all sectors of society for its unique health cultural connotation and excellent health care quality. By the end of 2009, it had won several awards from the National Cultural Heritage Administration and those of the municipal level.Now, it has become a business card for Hunan's external communication.

---

[11] Qianjin Pharmaceutical company, founded in 1966 and headquartered in Zhuzhou, Hunan Province, mainly produces CM. Qianjin series products are sold well across China. One of its flagship product, Fuke Qianjin Tablets, is a leading brand of oral Chinese medicine for gynecological inflammation.

天人合一维系

# 身心平衡

# The Unity of Heaven and Man Maintaining Physical and Mental Balance

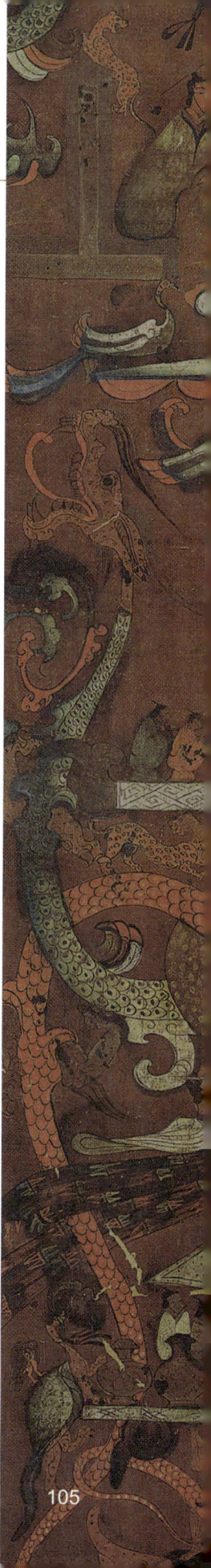

# 人与自然

　　大自然不仅是人类生命的萌芽地和繁衍地，更是人类身心的永久栖息地。古往今来，人们从大自然中获取赖以生存的丰富资源，亦在大自然里领略时空变迁的万千景象，获得美感、愉悦、放松、宁静、平和、活力等积极体验。然而，文明的进化与社会的发展使人类渐渐脱离了与大自然相统一的状态。个体化的历史进程让人们越来越远离大自然，失去了适应环境的本能，使现代人产生孤独感与隔绝感。对久居"钢筋水泥城堡"的人来说，长期缺乏与大自然的恰当接触，会产生焦虑、浮躁、厌倦、疲乏等负性体验。中国作为农耕文明的发源地，中国人天然地与大自然之间保持着亲密的联系，从而孕育了顺应自然、利用自然、保护自然的民族文化心理。对"人与自然"这个古老的命题来说，"天人合一"的整体观念是独属于东方的哲学智慧，它体现了中国古代宇宙观和生命观的独特内涵和价值，也深深影响和形塑了中医学的时空医学特色。

Nature is not only the cradle and breeding ground of human life, but also the permanent habitat of human body and spirit. Throughout history, people have obtained abundant resources necessary for survival from nature and also appreciated the wonder of countless changes in time and space within it, gaining positive experiences such as beauty, joy, safety, relaxation, tranquility, peace, and vitality. However, the evolution of civilization and the development of society have gradually led the human species away from a state of unity with nature. The historical process of individualization has made modern people increasingly dissociate from nature, losing the instinct to adapt to the environment and resulting in a feeling of loneliness and isolation. For those who long reside in "reinforced concrete castles", the lack of appropriate contact with nature for an extended period may bring them such negative feelings as anxiety, restlessness, boredom, fatigue, and loss. As the birthplace of agricultural civilization, China maintains a close connection with nature, thus nurturing a national cultural psychology of complying with nature, utilizing nature and protecting nature. For the ancient proposition of "human and nature", the holistic concept of "unity of heaven and man" has become a philosophy unique to the Orient. It highlights the unique connotations and values of ancient Chinese cosmology and philosophy of life, and deeply influences and shapes the temporal and spatial medical characteristics of CM.

# 人与自然

早在 2200 多年前，马王堆汉墓出土医书《十问》中就有这样的论述，书云："尔察天地之情，阴阳为正，万物失之而不继，得之而赢。"这段话的意思是，万物的运动变化（如花草树木的生长，日月的运动），都以天地阴阳为准则。如果违背这个规律，万物就不能生存、繁衍，适应这个规律万物就能兴旺发展。那么，人作为万物的灵长，其生长、善恶、寿夭与大自然之间又是怎样的关系呢？《十问》又云："君若欲寿，则顺察天地之道……君必察天地之请（情），而行之以身。"人要健康长寿，就必须了解天地自然的变化规律。只有通晓了这些自然规律，并按照规律身体力行就可长寿，而违背自然规律就有可能短命夭折。《十问》还介绍了顺应自然、聚精存神的方法，主张在没有征兆的情况下自然地蓄积能量，汲取天之甘露和瑶池之水以获得天地精气，保持深长呼吸使精气畅通，从而实现精神健旺。当然，这里的甘露、瑶泉泛指大自然中对身心有益的精华物质。

Written more than 2,200 years ago, the medical book *Ten Questions* unearthed from the Mawangdui Han Dynasty Tombs contains such a statement, "By observing heaven and earth, you find all follows the balance of yin and yang. Everything thrives with it and will not survive without it." In other words, the movement and changes of all things, including the growth of flowers, plants and trees, and the ability of the sun and moon to shine, follow the yin-yang balance principle of heaven and earth. Violating this law, nothing can survive or reproduce; adapting to it, they develop and become prosperous. That being so, what is the relationship between nature and the growth, morality, and life expectancy of human beings, the most intelligent in the world? The *Ten Questions* also states, "If you desire longevity, observe and follow the way of heaven and earth...You must observe the situations of heaven and earth and act accordingly." In order to be healthy and long-lived, one must understand the laws of natural changes. Only by understanding these laws and acting in accordance with them can one live a longer life, while going against them may lead to a premature death. The book also introduces methods of adapting to nature and preserving essence to harmonize spirit. It advocates natural accumulation without any signs, i.e., absorbing the dew of heaven and the water of the Yao Pool to obtain the essence of heaven and earth, and maintaining deep and long breaths to keep the essence flowing smoothly, so as to achieve mental vigor. The dew and the Yao Pool mentioned above are a generic term for beneficial essences of nature for the body and spirit.

　　辟谷作为一种天人合一的身心平衡之道，也是马王堆医学的独特贡献。在中国古代，"辟"通"避"，因此"辟谷"也被称为"却谷""休粮""绝粒"等，被视为一种祛除疾病、延年益寿之法。出土帛书《却谷食气》是迄今发现的最早记载辟谷服气术的著作，讲述了辟谷之人如何通过有节奏地呼吸大自然的"六气"，汲取日月精华，实现吐故纳新。《却谷食气》介绍了辟谷者服食石韦的方法，其一，要根据月的盈亏规律进行增减；其二，当出现头重脚轻、肢体发痛等不适时，应通过练气功使不适缓解。那么，辟谷时的"六气"又分别指什么呢？第一种气叫"朝霞"，出现在清晨太阳即将从地平线升起之时；第二种气叫"输阳"，出现在上午七八点；第三种气叫"正阳"，出现在中午 12 点；第四种气叫"铣光"，出现于午后太阳被密云遮蔽的场合；第五种气叫"输阴"，出现于傍晚太阳落至地平线后；第六种气叫"沆瀣"，出现于夜间 12 点。"食气"即将静坐、存想等身心调摄之术融入与大自然的亲密接触之中，生动地反映了中国古人天人合一的整体观念。

As a way of balancing body and spirit through the unity of heaven and man, "辟谷 (avoiding grains)" is also a unique contribution of Mawangdui medicine. In ancient Chinese, the character "辟" has a sense of "避 (avoiding)". Therefore, "辟谷" is also called "却谷 (refusing grains)", "休粮 (avoiding food)", and "绝粒 (cutting off food)". It was regarded as a method of eliminating diseases and extending life. The unearthed book on silk, the *Avoiding Food Intake and Practising Breathing to Cultivate Qi*, is the earliest record of avoiding grains and consuming qi practice discovered so far. It describes how practitioners of avoiding grains inhale the "six qi" of nature rhythmically, absorb the essence of the sun and moon, and achieve rejuvenation. The book introduces how practitioners of avoiding grains take Shiwei (Folium Pyrrosiae). First, increase or decrease the amount according to the waxing and waning of the moon; second, perform qi exercises to relieve dizziness and limb pain when they occur. And what do the "six qi" that are consumed during the period of avoiding grains refer to? They are called "morning glow", "rising sun", "midday sun", "bright light", "setting sun", and "night aura", which appear respectively when the sun is about to rise from the horizon (morning glow), around seven or eight o'clock in the morning (rising sun), at noon (midday sun), when the sun is obscured by dense clouds in the afternoon (bright light), in the evening after the sun has set below the horizon (setting sun), and at midnight (night aura). "Inhaling qi" integrates the method of adjusting body and spirit such as sitting quietly, cultivating and regulating qi into intimate contact with nature, which vividly reflects the ancient Chinese concept of the unity of heaven and man.

马王堆三号墓出土帛书《却谷食气》《阴阳十一脉灸经》（乙本），以及《导引图》
Silk Manuscript of the *Avoiding Food Intake and Practicing Breathing to Cultivate Qi*, the *Moxibustion Classic of the Eleven Yin-Yang Meridians* (Version B), and the *Drawings of Guiding and Stretching in Tomb 3*

马王堆医学中的身心平衡之道，不仅体现为"天人合一"的养生智慧，还充分表现为"存神"的心理养生思想。《十问》曰："心制死生，孰为之败？慎守勿失，长生累世。"这里指出要管理心念，节欲保精才能长寿。《十问》又曰："神和内得，云（魂）柏（魄）皇□（□表示缺字），五臧（脏）轼（固）白（薄），玉色重光，寿参日月，为天地英。"再次强调要保持神和内得，精神和谐，才能精力充沛，内脏坚固健壮，容颜青春焕发，健康长寿，成为身体素质很强的人。作为独具特色的医学思想，马王堆医学中的心身医学被学界概括为三个方面，即心身合一的养生观、心身合参的疾病观、心身结合的治疗法。比如马王堆导引术作为养生功法，将意念训练、呼吸吐纳和形体锻炼相结合，可谓心身合一、形神共养。而《足臂十一脉灸经》将情志症状纳入疾病临床诊断，并认为据此可以推断疾病的吉凶善恶，体现了心神合参的疾病观。治疗方面，祝由疗法、静心宁神等身心协调方法散见于马王堆医书之中。"存神"思想的核心内涵可归纳为三个层面：一

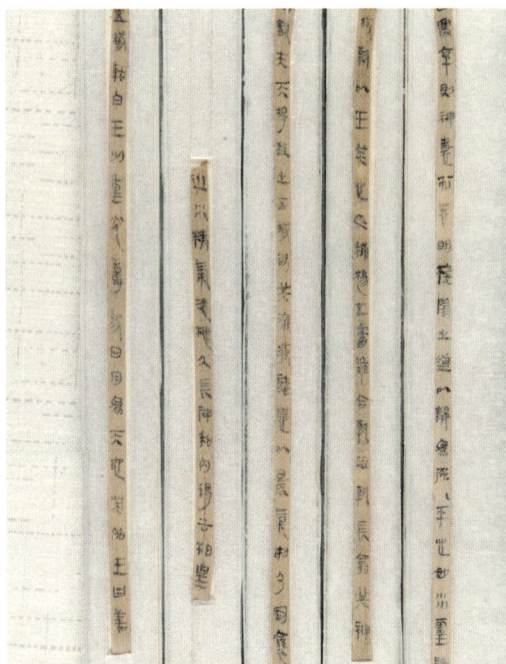

马王堆三号墓出土医简《十问》记载"存神"思想的原文（局部图）
The Original Text Describing the Concept of "Preserving the Spirit" from the *Ten Questions* on Bamboo Strips in Tomb 3 (Partial Picture)

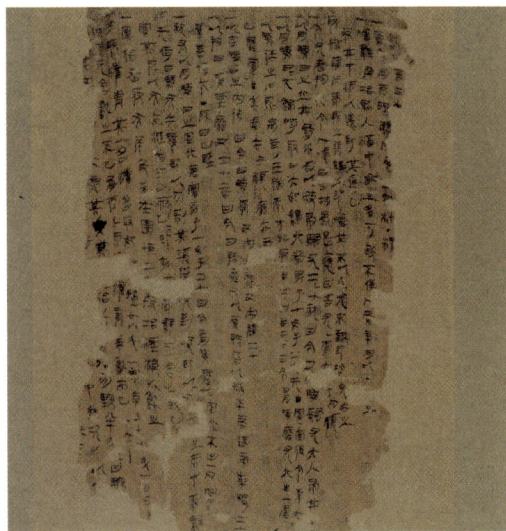

马王堆三号墓出土医书《五十二病方》记载祝由方的原文（局部图）
The Original Text Describing Zhuyou Therapy from the *Formulas for Fifty-two Diseases* in Tomb 3 (Partial Picture)

The way of physical and mental balance in Mawangdui medicine is not only reflected in the health preservation wisdom of "the unity of heaven and man", but is also fully demonstrated in the psychological health concept of "harmonizing spirit".The *Ten Questions* states,"The spirit can govern life and death; what causes its failure? Carefully guard and do not lose it, and you will live a long life through ages." This indicates that managing thoughts and moderating desires to preserve essence can lead to longevity. The book also states, "A peaceful temperament and an inner fulfillment will naturally ensure abundant energy and vibrant spirit; when the five zang organs are full of essence and blood, one will naturally have a radiant appearance, be full of joy, be able to enjoy a long lifespan like the sun and moon, thus becomes the elite among all living creatures in the world." It re-emphasizes the importance of maintaining peace and achieving inner fulfillment, harmonizing the spirit to attain vitality, ensuring the five zang organs are strong and healthy, preserving a youthful appearance, securing longevity, and strengthening the body. As a set of unique medical thoughts, the achievements of psychosomatic medicine covered in Mawangdui medical books are summarized by academia in three aspects: the concept of health preservation that unites body and spirit, the view of disease that integrates body and spirit, and the treatment method that combines body and spirit. For example, Mawangdui Daoyin Technique, as a health-preserving exercise, combines spirit training, breathing exercises, and physical exercise, creating a harmonious blend of body, and fostering the simultaneous nourishement of both the physical form and inner spirit. The *Moxibustion Classic of the Eleven Meridians of the Foot and Forearm* illustrates emotional symptoms to diagnose diseases, and believes that it can be used to infer the good and evil, auspicious and inauspicious nature of diseases, reflecting its views on disease that combine body and spirit. In terms of treatment, methods such as Zhuyou therapy and calming the mind and spirit, which harmonize body and spirit, are scattered throughout Mawangdui medical books. The core connotation of the "harmonizing spirit" thought can be summarized into three aspects: First, the laws of natural change must be followed so that "all things are able to thrive" and the spirit lasts forever. This means to comply with the laws of nature, follow the way of yin-yang changes in heaven and earth, and adjust diet, daily life and emotions according to natural rhythms such as the waxing and waning of the sun and moon, the alteration from day to night, and the change of the four seasons. Second, peace between the spirit and the physical form must be achieved and the spirit and will must be united so that the soul and spirit are kept within. The *Ten Questions* says, "Breathing in the evening should be deep, long and slow, so that the ears cannot hear the sound of it in order to help sleep. This way, the soul and spirit are tranquil, thus promoting longevity." This means that breathing in the evening should be deep, slow, and gentle, which is conducive to sleep, and in this way the spirit is at peace in the form, which can lead to a long life. The book also says, "Once lost in one night, sleep will not be compensated for a hundred days...Therefore, those who understand the

要遵循自然变化规律，才能使"万物得继"，神长存。即顺应自然规律，遵循天地阴阳变化之道，根据日月消长、昼夜晨昏、四季变化等自然节律来调摄饮食、起居及情志各方面。二要做到神形相安、神志相合，使魂魄内守。《十问》曰："暮息之志，深息长除，使耳勿闻，且以安寝。魂魄安形，故能长生。"意思是，夜间的呼吸吐纳要深长徐缓，利于安眠，这样精神安于形体就能长生长寿。《十问》又曰："一昔（夕）不卧，百日不复……故道者敬卧。"再次强调了睡眠状态下心神屈藏而止息，魂魄相合而安宁，魂不游荡而无梦，魄处其舍而形静，对个体的身心休养十分重要。三要做到喜怒制神以存神。《十问》曰："彼生有殃，必其阴精漏泄，百脉菀废，喜怒不时，不明大道，生气去之。"此处明确提出了"喜怒"（即情志因素）在疾病发生发展过程中的意义，纵欲过度可致阴精漏泄、精衰气竭，全身经脉就会郁闭不通，因而表现出喜怒无常，由于不懂得养生之根本大道，使精神生机离自身而去。此外，马王堆医书中还载有祝由方 40 多条，主要集中在《五十二病方》《养生方》《房内记》《杂禁方》四篇医书当中，体现了当时通过"移精变气"来调摄身心、治疗疾病的特殊方法。

methods of maintaining health value sleep." It once again emphasizes the importance of the mind and spirit being hidden and resting during sleep, the soul and spirit being at peace and tranquil, the soul not wandering and without dreams, and the spirit staying in its place while the form is still, which are very important for physical and mental cultivation. Third, control one's emotions to harmonize the spirit within. Besides, the book says, "If there is a disaster in life, it must be due to the leakage of yin essence, and the meridians are in disrepair. As a result, one becomes moody, obeys the way of health preservation, and loses vitality." Here, it clearly points out the significance of "joy and anger"—emotional factors—in the process of disease occurrence and development. Indulgence in excessive desires can lead to leakage of yin essence and exhaustion of essence and energy, thus all the meridians will be blocked, and one will become moody. This reflects a lack of understanding of the fundamental way of health preservation, leading to the depletion of one's spirit and vitality. In addition, Mawangdui medical books also contain more than 40 Zhuyou formulas. They are mainly recorded in the *Formulas for Fifty-two Diseases,* the *Formulas for Health Preservation,* the *Formulas for Sexual Life,* and the *Formulas for Various Charms,* reflecting the special methods of adjusting the body and spirit and treating diseases by "transforming the essence to qi" at that time.

概而言之，养生必先养心，而养心的本质是养神，养心"存神"是维持身心平衡的要旨。生活在物质文明高度发达的现代，先进的科学技术让我们的生活越来越依赖于外物，我们的肢体也利用得越来越少。我们把手脚解放出来，却让头脑充斥着海量信息，远离自然，远离生态，蜗居在情感疏离的物质空壳，远离青山绿水，也就远离了健康长寿之道。中国古人"天人合一"的思想观念，蕴含着身心平衡的健康密码。马王堆医学所蕴含的跨越千年的生态智慧，能够滋养和开启我们的美好心情，为我们带来独特的体验和收获。

In general, to preserve health, one should begin by nourishing the spirit, which essentially means nurturing the spirit; the primary purpose of maintaining physical and mental balance is to harmonize spirit through nourishing the heart. As we live in a modern society with highly developed material civilization, our lives are increasingly dependent on external objects due to advanced science and technology, and we use our limbs less and less. Human nature is becoming more and more blinded by industrial civilization, with less and less physical activity. While we free our hands and feet, our minds are filled with massive amounts of information, distancing us from nature, ecology, and living in an emotionally disconnected material shell. Keeping away from green mountains and rivers and from our natural instincts means drifting away from physical and mental health, and deviating from the path to longevity and health. The ancient Chinese concept of "unity of heaven and man" contains the health code for a balanced body and spirit. The ecological wisdom from Mawangdui medicine, spanning over a thousand years, brings a unique experience and harvest for nourishing and enlightening our wonderful moods.

房中养生稳固

# 两性和谐

# The Sexual Health Preservation
# Stabilizing Marital Harmony

　　两性结合作为一种最基本的性别复合与弥补，是人类社会繁衍生息的前提。《周易·序卦》曰："有天地然后有万物，有万物然后有男女，有男女然后有夫妇，有夫妇然后有父子，有父子然后有君臣，有君臣然后有上下，有上下然后礼义有所错。"此即主张人类社会的父子、君臣、兄弟、朋友等一切人伦关系都是由夫妇的结合而派生出来的。中国儒家将夫妇关系视为"人伦之始""五代之基"，指出"君子之道，造端乎夫妇"，乃为"大论"。性爱作为夫妻关系的基础，也是人类共通的生理本能和基本需求。美国著名社会心理学家马斯洛的需要层次理论指出，性和水、食物一样，是强烈的、不可避免的最底层的基本需要。如果性的需要长期得不到满足，就会引起个体的身心失衡和紧张，从而对身体健康、人格发展等产生不利影响。因此，科学和谐的性爱不仅具备情感和行为上的双重审美价值，还对人的身心健康具有重要意义。

The union of male and female, as the most fundamental form of gender complementarily and reconciliation, serves as a prerequisite for the reproduction and continuation of human society. According to the "Sequential Hexagrams" chapter in the *Book of Changes*, "With the existence of heaven and earth, all beings came into being, giving rise to the distinction between male and female, which in turn led to the emergence of husbands and wives. Consequently, parent-child relationships were formed, followed by the establishment of rulers and ministers, ultimately defining the hierarchy of high and low status." This suggests that all human relationships, such as parent-child, ruler-minister, siblings, and friends, stem from the matrimony of husband and wife. Confucianism views the relationship between husband and wife as "the beginning of human relationships" and "the foundation of generations"; it points out that "the way of a gentleman starts with the relationship between husband and wife," which is considered a "major principle." Sexual love, as the foundation of the marital relationship, is also a common physiological instinct and basic need of human beings. The hierarchy of needs theory proposed by the American social psychologist Maslow holds that sex, like water and food, is a strong and inevitable basic need at the lowest level. If this need for sexual intimacy is not satisfied over time, it may lead to imbalance and tension in an individual, thereby negatively impacting physical health, personality development, and overall well-being. Therefore, scientific harmonious sexual intercourse not only has dual aesthetic value in terms of emotional and behavioral aspects, but also holds significant importance for an individual's physical and mental health.

# 马王堆

由于文化禁忌的影响，关于性的科学研究，无论东方还是西方，都走过一段漫长的历史。即便是在历史文化传统更为开放的西方，性医学的真正研究也仅始于一个多世纪以前。比如，有的观点认为，西方最早开展性研究的是英国医生艾利斯，他致力于剖析复杂的人类性行为，尤其对非典型性性行为的个体进行了大量研究。有的观点指出，美国医生马斯特斯和约翰逊完成了性医学这门学科的创立工作，其著述的《人类性反应》出版于1966年。然而，随着马王堆汉墓出土医书中多部性医学典籍的面世，性医学研究的起点有了更为久远的溯源。出土竹简《十问》《合阴阳》《天下至道谈》，是迄今发现的最早的房中养生专著。而《养生方》《房内记》《杂禁方》《胎产书》等出土帛书中也含有大量性医学内容，尤其是《十问》的出土，填补了中国汉代以前性医学文献的空白，为中国性医学研究提供了极其珍贵的资料。

马王堆三号墓出土医简《十问》
The *Ten Questions* on Bamboo Strips in Tomb 3

Due to the profound impact of cultural taboos, scientific research on human sexuality has traversed a lengthy and complex history in both Eastern and Western cultures. Even in the West, where historical and cultural traditions are generally more open-minded, the genuine study of sexual medicine did not begin until over a century ago. For instance, some scholars attribute the earliest sexual research in the West to British physician Henry H. Ellis (1859—1939), who devoted himself to analyzing intricate human sexual behaviors, with a particular focus on individuals exhibiting atypical sexual behaviors. Others argue that American physicians William H. Masters (1915—2001) and Virginia E. Johnson (1925—2013) pioneered the discipline of sexology, and as evidenced by their seminal work *Human Sexual Response* published in 1966. However, with the recent excavation of numerous ancient medical classics from the Mawangdui Han Dynasty Tombs, it has become increasingly clear that the origins of sexual medicine research date back even further. Among these discoveries are the *Ten Questions*, the *Conjoining Yin and Yang*, and the *Discussion on the Supreme Dao of the World* written on bamboo slips, which represent the earliest known works on preserving sexual health to date. Furthermore, ancient silk books on silk-such as the *Formulas for Health Preservation*, the *Formulas for Sexual Life*, the *Formulas for Various Charms*, and the *Book of Obstetrics* also extensively cover various aspects of sexual medicine.The excavation of the *Ten Questions* in particular has filled a significant gap in Chinese sexual medical literature prior to the Han Dynasty in China, providing invaluable material for the researchers seeking to understand the history and development of Chinese sexual medicine.

中国古人将夫妻之间的性交合活动称为"接阴之道""房中之术"。虽然中国历史上经历过种种"谈性变色"的时代，但是房事养生一直作为一个严肃、严谨的命题在历史变迁中得到延续和拓展。中国先哲在房事养生学的研究中取得了辉煌的成就，其中许多理论和实践在今天仍有其先进性和科学性。马王堆医学中的房事养生思想与方法是中国古代性医学的典型代表。通过史料研究发现，先秦两汉时期的养生学家对房中术的态度是非常严肃的。他们将房中养生视为健康长寿的基础，认为人既要享受房事之乐，又要有所节制，这样就可以气血平和、生命长久，反之则可能导致疾病，甚至断送性命。那么，同时期的马王堆房事养生思想，又有哪些特色观点呢？

In ancient China, the sexual activities between husband and wife were referred to as "the way of yin union" and "the art in the bedroom". Despite the fact that sex was a taboo topic in various periods in Chinese history, the concept of health preservation through sexual activities has always been treated with seriousness and rigor. Ancient Chinese philosophers have made brilliant achievements in the study of sexual health, and many of their theories and practices remain advanced and scientific today. The "sexual health preservation" thoughts and methods in Mawangdui medicine are a typical representation of of ancient Chinese sexual medicine. Historical studies reveal that health preservation experts in the Pre-Qin and Han dynasties had a very serious attitude towards sexual activities, viewing them as the foundation for good health and longevity. They believed that one should not only enjoy the pleasures of sex but also exercise restraint, which can lead to a balanced flow of qi and blood, and a long life; otherwise, one may fall ill or even die. And what are the features and views of Mawangdui sexual health preservation thoughts in the same period?

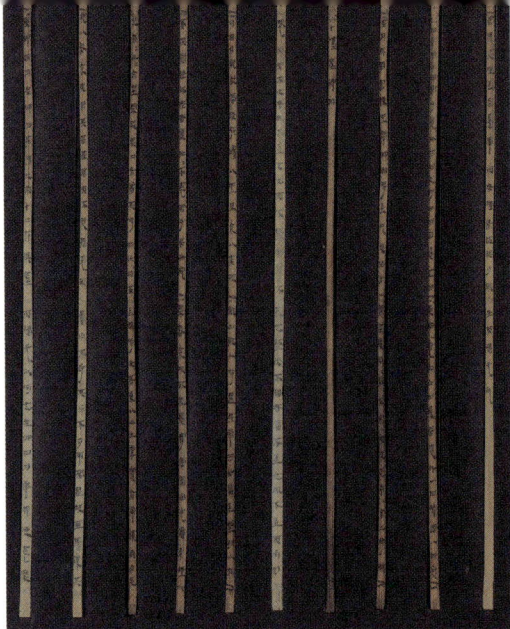

马王堆三号墓出土医简《天下
至道谈》
The *Discussion on the Supreme Dao
of the World* on Bamboo Strips in
Tomb 3

马王堆房事养生思想的一个重要内容，就是揭示了"夫妻性福和谐有指征"。由于受到当时道家文化的影响，马王堆医学文化具有典型的"重阴"色彩，因而在房事养生中也非常注重女性的作用，流露出对女性性生理和性心理的关注和重视。出土医书中对女性的性兴奋和性高潮做了深入观察和细致研究，认为女性性兴奋和性高潮主要表现为"五音""十征"等，丈夫可以根据这些不同的表现来适应配偶所处的兴奋阶段，满足妻子的性心理渴求，这是达到性生活和谐幸福的关键所在。比如，《天下至道谈》云："五言（音），一曰候（喉）息，二曰喘（喘）息，三曰累哀，四曰疢，五曰龄，审察五言，以智（知）其心；审察八动，以知其所乐所通。"意思是说，性交合过程中，女子性兴奋时会不由自主发出五种呼吸及娇嗔感叹声，丈夫通过仔细观察这五种声音，可了解妻子的性兴奋及性高潮程度，并知道妻子对性交合的心理反应和需求。而《合阴阳》中进一步谈到了女子性交合过程中的"十征"，即从性兴奋逐渐达到性高潮的十种不同的性心理、生理反应过程。如果能够配合"十征"把握性交合的时机，则有利于保持旺盛的精神和敏锐的言行，有益于男女身心健康。《合阴阳》还论述了男子性交合方式的"十势"和女子在性交合过程中的"八动"，通过把握女子性心理渴求的八种特征和男子性交合的十种姿势，满足双方的性心理和性生理需求，实现夫妻身心健康和家庭幸福。

One significant aspect of Mawangdui sexual health preservation thoughts lies in the notion that "there are indicators of harmony and satisfaction in marital sex." Under the influence of contemporary Daoist culture, Mawangdui medical thought exhibits a distinctive emphasis on the feminine perspective in sexual health preservation, demonstrating a keen awareness of women's sexual physiology and psychology. The unearthed medical texts provide detailed observations and research on women's sexual arousal and orgasm, which manifest themselves primarily through "five sounds" and "ten signs". By paying close attention to these varied expressions, husbands can adapt their approach to meet their spouses' evolving levels of arousal, thereby satisfying their spouses' sexual and psychological needs. This is the key to achieving a harmonious and fulfilling marital sex life. For instance, the *Discussion on the Supreme Dao of the World* states, "There are five sounds—breathing, panting, lamenting, moaning and gnawing.By listening to these five sounds, one can discern their heart; by observing their movements, one can and understand their joy or pain." This implies that during the process of sexual intercourse, women in arousal will involuntarily produce five distinctive types of breaths and coquettish sighs. By carefully observing these sounds, husbands can gain insight into their wives' levels of arousal and orgasm, as well as their psychological responses and desires. The *Conjoining Yin and Yang* further elaborates the "ten signs" that women exhibit during the process of sexual intercourse, i.e., 10distinct stages of gradual progression from arousal to orgasm. By grasping the timing of sexual intercourse through these "ten signs", individuals can benefit their physical and mental health, preserving their vitality and vigor. The book also explores the concept of male "ten postures" and female "eight movements" in the process of sexual intercourse. By understanding and mastering these eight movement characteristics of female psychological desires and the 10 postures of males, couples can better satisfy each other's sexual requirements, ultimately achieving their physical and mental well-being, as well as the happiness of their family.

马王堆三号墓出土医简《合阴阳》
The *Conjoining Yin and Yang* on Bamboo Strips in Tomb 3

马王堆房事养生思想对我国房事养生学理论的重大贡献，还在于"七损八益"的论述，提出了性活动中的适宜法则和不宜做法。《天下至道谈》说道："气有八益，有七损。不能用八益去七损，则行年四十而有阴气自半也，五十而起居衰，六十而耳目不聪明，七十下枯上竭，阴气不用，深泣留（流）出。令之复壮有道，去七损以抵其病，用八益以补其气，是故老者复壮，壮不衰。"它指出，在男女性交合活动中有八种对人体精气起补益作用和有利于保持身心健康的做法，有七种对人体精气和身心健康起耗损作用的做法。如果在性交合过程中不善于运用"七损八益"原则来调整行为，则会出现年龄未过 40 岁而阴精亏损，未老先衰，50 岁就行动不便，60岁即耳聋眼花，70 岁时阳气衰竭，生殖系统萎缩干枯，性心理、生理活动衰退，不能再进行性交合活动。身体精神保持年轻、防治疾患的方法就是要在性交合过程中遵循"七损八益"原则，使体内虚损的精气得以充盈，这样可使已衰弱的老年人恢复健壮，使性机能处于旺盛时期的青壮年不会过早衰老。《十问》中对"八益"和"七损"进行了详细阐释，并强调在性交合中进行气功导引可以调理精血之气，增强补益作用。《十问》提出的"七损八益"房中养生术对后世的性保健有着深远影响，也得到了后世医家的不断丰富完善。

The significant contributions to China's sexual health preservation studies made by Mawangdui sexual health preservation thoughts also lie in their discussions on "seven losses and eight benefits", which proposes the dos and don'ts for sexual activities. The *Discussion on the Supreme Dao of the World* records, "There are eight benefits and seven losses in qi. If one cannot use the benefits to counteract the losses, then by 40, their physiological functions will decrease by half; by 50, their mobility will decline; by 60, their vision and hearing will weaken; by 70, their lower body will dry up, their upper body will weaken, their sexual organs will lose their function, and deep sorrow will be left behind. To restore vigor to the body, one must eliminate the seven losses that lead to illnesses and use the eight benefits to tonify qi, allowing the elderly to regain vitality and delay aging. It highlights that during sexual intercourse, there are eight practices that have nourishing effects on essence and qi and on physical and mental health, while seven practices have negative effects on them. If one fails to apply the principle of "seven losses and eight benefits" in adjusting behavior during sexual activities, it may lead to premature aging before 40, difficulty in movement at 50, deafness and blurred vision at 60, and yang qi exhaustion at 70, resulting in the withering of the reproductive system and decline in psychosexual and physiological activities. To maintain a youthful body and spirit, prevent and treat diseases, restore vitality, one must follow the principle of "seven losses and eight benefits" during the process of sexual intercourse, replenishing the depleted essence and qi in the body, enabling the elderly who have weakened to regain their strength, and preventing young and middle-aged individuals in their prime from aging prematurely. The elaborations on "eight benefits" and "seven losses" in the *Ten Questions* emphasize that qi exercise and daoyin during intercourse can regulate the essence and blood, enhancing the nourishing effects. These discussions on sexual health preservation have had a profound impact on future generations and have been enriched and improved by later generations of medical practitioners.

马王堆房事养生还提出了许多性保健的原则，至今仍有指导意义。如《天下至道谈》说："故贰生者食也，孙（损）生者色也，是以圣人合男女必有则也。"男女性交合必须遵循哪些原则呢？《天下至道谈》认识到，要使夫妻双方在性交合中保持身心健康，必须在夫妻双方情意绵绵、难舍难分时，在轻松愉快的气氛中进行性交合活动。同时，交合之道"以静为强"。正如《十问》云："棱（接）阴之道，以静为强，平心如水，灵路（露）内臟（藏），款以玉筴（策），心毋秋（怵）（荡），五音进合（答）……致之五臟（藏），欲其深臓（藏）。"在夫妻性生活时，心境安静是最重要的，心情坦荡如水，则阴精内藏而不外溢。对于现代人而言，正确认识自身的性生理和性心理需要，保持内心坦荡，做好科学的节育避孕工作，将有利于保持良好的心境状态，不被担心或恐惧的情绪所干扰。当然，也不能恣意放肆自己的性欲，要根据双方的情绪调动水平和生理反应差异调整节奏。更为重要的是要避免房劳，马王堆房事养生强调守精延寿，认为节制性生活就能收到"行年百岁，贤于往者"的效果，尤其倡导动而不泄，从而起到固护肾精、还精补脑、祛病延年的作用。

In Mawangdui sexual health preservation thoughts, many principles are proposed for maintaining sexual health. They are still of guiding significance today. For example, the *Discussion on the Supreme Dao of the World* notes, "Food sustains life, while improper sexual activities can harm it. Hence, a sage must follow certain principles in sexual matters." Then, what are the principles of sexual intercourse? The book recognizes that to maintain physical and mental health during sexual intercourse, both partners should engage in the activity with deep emotional connection and a relaxed, pleasant mood...Moreover, as emphasized in the way of sexual intercourse, "stillness is strength." As the *Ten Questions* advises, "The way of sexual intercourse stresses stillness as strength, keeping a calm and tranquil state of mind like water. This allows the essence and energy to be stored deep within the body, unaffected by external stimuli. One should stimulate the female's genitals with the penis, avoid panic or indulgence, and listen to the five sounds...transporting them to the five zang organs, where they can be stored away." A quiet mind is essential during sexual intercourse, as it helps maintain the essence internal without leakage. For modern individuals, having a proper understanding of their own sexual physiology and psychology is crucial. Keeping an open mind and taking scientific contraceptive measures can help preserve a good mental state,free from worries or fears. It is also essential not to indulge in sexual desires, but to adjust the pace according to both parties' emotional and physiological differences. More importantly, it is necessary to avoid excessive sexual activity. Mawangdui sexual health preservation thoughts emphasize preserving essence for longevity, believing that controlling sexual life can achieve the effect of "living to a hundred years old, and being wiser than the former generations." They particularly advocate for moving without exhausting oneself so as to nourish and protect kidney, leaving the essence to nourish brain, expel diseases, and prolong life.

马王堆医学中的性医学思想只是古老的东方性医学宝库的一隅，建立在中国古代阴阳学说基础上的性医学，构成了中医药防病治病思想中的一道特色风景线。由于受到社会文化、习俗及生活方式等多方面的影响，中医性医学思想的科学挖掘和传承弘扬还远远不够。随着中医药事业的振兴发展，以及社会文明的不断前进，深信源远流长的中医性医学必定能以自身的特色理论与实践，为人类的性医学及优生学等领域做出更大贡献。

马王堆三号墓出土医简
《杂禁方》
The *Formulas for Various Charms* on Bamboo Strips in Tomb 3

The sexual medical thoughts in Mawangdui medicine represent a fragment of the ancient Eastern treasure trove of sexual knowledge. Built upon the foundation of traditional Chinese yin-yang theory, sexology has become an integral part of the unique ideological landscape of Chinese medicine. Despite its rich cultural heritage and historical significance, the scientific exploration and inheritance of Chinese sexual medicine ideology remain woefully underdeveloped due to the complex interplay of social, cultural, and lifestyle factors. However, with the revitalization and growth of CM, as well as the steady progress of social civilization, there is growing evidence that the long-standing traditions of Chinese sexual medicine will definitely make greater contributions to fields of human sexual medicine and eugenics. Its distinctive theoretical frameworks and practical applications offer a unique perspective on these complex issues, one that is both rooted in ancient wisdom and attuned to modern needs.

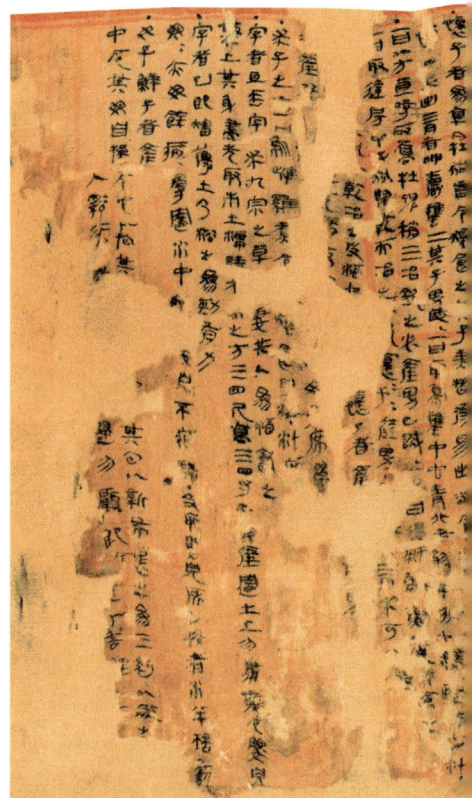

马王堆三号墓出土帛书《胎产书》
Silk Manuscript of the *Book of Obstetrics* in Tomb 3

131

# 结束语

# Concluding Remarks

在这趟探索马王堆医学文化的奇妙之旅中，我们仿佛穿越了千年的时光，走进了古老东方智慧的殿堂。这里，不仅有医学的瑰宝，更蕴藏着古人对生命与健康的深刻领悟。马王堆医学文化以其深厚的文化底蕴和独特的医学理念，展现了中华民族对生命健康的积极追求和独到见解。

马王堆汉墓的发现，如同打开了一扇窗，让我们得以窥见马王堆医学文化的博大精深。从经脉学说的源远流长，到出土竹简中的饮食智慧；从《导引图》中古人与能量的和谐互动，到那些防病治病的草药与香料的独特功效；从房中养生的两性和谐之道，到起居调摄的健康追求；从聚精、养气、存神的健康理念，再到"天人合一"的哲学思想。马王堆医学文化，不仅是一部医学宝典，更是一种生活的艺术，它教导我们在自然中寻找和谐，在纷扰的生活中寻求身心的平衡与健康。

In this fascinating journey of exploration into Mawangdui medical culture, we seem to traverse centuries, entering the grand hall of ancient Oriental wisdom. Here, not only are there treasures of medicine, but also the profound and timeless insights that Chinese ancestors had gained about life and health. The Mawangdui medical culture, with its rich cultural heritage and unique medical concepts, exemplifies the Chinese people's relentless pursuit of a deeper understanding of life and health.

The discovery of Mawangdui Han Dynasty Tombs, allowing us to glimpse of the richness and profoundness of the Mawangdui medical culture: from the centuries-old roots of meridian theory to the dietary wisdom revealed in unearthed bamboo boxes; from the harmonious interaction between ancient people and energy depicted in the *Drawings of Guiding and Stretching* to the enigmatic powers of medicinal herbs and spices for disease prevention and treatment; from the principle of harmony in maintaining sexual health to the pursuit of health through adjustments in daily living habits; from the healthy ideals of preserving essence, cultivating qi, and harmonizing spirit to the illuminating philosophical concept of "the unity between heaven and man." The Mawangdui medical culture is not only a comprehensive medical encyclopedia, but also an art of living that teaches us how to find balance within nature, and how to cultivate physical and mental equilibrium amidst life's turmoil.

　　这份跨越千年的医学智慧，在中国古代社会中发挥了不可磨灭的作用，在科技迅猛发展的今日，它依然闪耀着不可替代的价值和光芒。它提醒我们，真正的健康不仅源自身体的力量，更源自心灵的平和；真正的养生，不仅是对疾病的治疗，更是对生命的尊重与呵护。

　　马王堆医学文化的智慧，不仅属于中国，更属于全世界。随着全球化的不断深入，越来越多的国际学者被这份古老的医学遗产吸引，他们试图从中汲取智慧，寻找解决现代健康问题的灵感。马王堆医学文化以其独特的魅力，架起了一座连接东西方医学的桥梁，促进了不同文化之间的交流与融合。

　　我们期待，这份古老的医学遗产能够在现代社会焕发出新的光彩，为全人类的健康事业贡献更多的智慧和力量。愿马王堆医学文化的精髓，如同一股生生不息的清泉，引领我们走向一个更加健康、和谐的未来。

This millennium-old medical wisdom has left an indelible mark on ancient Chinese society, yet its value and significance remain unparalleled in today's fast-paced scientific and technological era. It serves as a poignant reminder that true health is not solely derived from physical prowess, but also from the harmony of mind; and that true health preservation extends far beyond disease treatment to encompass a profound respect and care for life itself.

The wisdom of Mawangdui medical culture is a treasure not only for China but for humanity as a whole. As globalization continues to evolve, this ancient medical heritage has been attracting more and more international scholars seeking to unlock its secrets and tap into its wisdom to address health challenges of modern times. The Mawangdui medical culture, by virtue of its unique allure, has forged a bridge between East and West, facilitating cross-cultural exchange and integration in the realm of medicine.

It is our hope that this ancient medical heritage will once again shine brightly in modern society, illuminating new paths to better health and well-being for all humanity. May the essence of the Mawangdui medical culture continue to flow like a crystal-clear spring, guiding us towards a future characterized by harmony, balance, and optimal wellness.